The Meaning of the Church

THE MEANING OF THE CHURCH

Romano Guardini

Translated from the German
VOM SINN DER KIRCHE
by Ada Lane

CLUNY MEDIA

Cluny Media edition, 2018

For more information regarding this title
or any other Cluny Media publication,
please write to info@clunymedia.com, or to
Cluny Media, P.O. Box 1664, Providence, RI, 02901

ISBN: 978-1944418991

Nihil obstat:
Innocentius Apap, O.P., S.T.M., *Censor deputatus*

Imprimatur:
✠ Joseph Butt, *Vic. Gen.*

Westmonasterii, *die* 27 Iulii 1935

The Nihil obstat *and* Imprimatur *are a declaration that a book
or pamphlet is considered to be free from doctrinal or moral error.
It is not implied that those who have granted the* Nihil obstat *and*
Imprimatur *agree with the contents, opinions or statements expressed.*

Cover design by Clarke & Clarke
Cover image: Jan van Eyck, *The Last Judgment* (detail),
c. 1440–1441, oil on canvas, transferred from wood
Courtesy of The Metropolitan Museum of Art, New York

Contents

I.   The Awakening of the Church in the Soul   1

II.   The Church and Personality   27

III. The Way to Become Human   49

IV.   The Road to Freedom   71

V.   Community   101

      Epilogue   127

I. The Awakening of the Church in the Soul

A religious process of incalculable importance has begun—the Church is coming to life in the souls of men.

This must be correctly understood. The Church has, of course, been continuously alive in herself, and at all times of decisive importance for her members. They have accepted her teaching, obeyed her commands; her invincible vitality has been their strong support and the ground of their trust. But, with the development of individualism since the end of the Middle Ages, the Church has been thought of as a means to true religious life—a God-designed framework or vessel in which that life is contained—a viaduct of life but not as life itself.[1] It has, in other words, been thought of as a thing exterior from which men might receive life, not a thing into which men must be incorporated that they

1

may live with its life. Religious life tended increasingly away from the community and towards the individual sphere. The Church, therefore, came to be regarded as the boundary of this sphere, and perhaps even as its opponent. In any case the Church was felt as a power fettering personality and thereby restricting the religious life. And this external regulation appeared either beneficent, or inevitable, or oppressive, according to the disposition of the individual.

This is inevitably a one-sided presentation. Actually there were very many exceptions; transition and development made the picture far more complicated. Nor was this attitude to the Church without its greatness. Today all the catchwords of the age are against it; but we should ask nevertheless what valuable contributions it has made to religious life as a whole. Perhaps it is the right moment to do so, just because we inwardly stand apart from it and can therefore look at it objectively.

What was the basis of this attitude? The answer has already been indicated—the subjectivism and individualism of the modern age.

Religion was considered as something which belonged to the subjective sphere—it was simply something within a man, a condition of his soul. We are not speaking of conscious scientific theories, but of the spiritual tendency of the age. Objective religion represented by the Church was for the individual primarily the regulation of this individual and subjective religion; a protection against its inadequacies. That which remained over and above—the objective religion in its disinterested sublimity, and the community as a value in itself often left the individual cold and aroused no response in his heart. Even the acceptance and the enthusiasm which the Church evoked were largely external and individualistic, and psychologically had a strong affinity with the earlier "patriotism."

When we look more closely we see that often enough there was no genuine belief in the existence of objective religious realities. This subjectivism dominated religious life all through the second half of the nineteenth century and during the beginning of the twentieth. Man felt imprisoned within himself. That is why from Kant onwards, and particularly in the more recent idealism, the problem of knowledge became so urgent—indeed for many it constituted the whole of philosophy. The man of this age considered the very existence of an object as doubtful. He was not directly and strongly conscious of the reality of things, at bottom indeed not even of his own. Such intellectual systems as consistent solipsism did not rest upon logical conclusions, but were tentative interpretations of this personal experience. It is impossible to explain on purely intellectual grounds such philosophies as the new idealism for which the subject is a mere logical entity. They arose from the attempt to replace the

3

objective reality of things, which had become doubtful, by a logical reality. Thus originated the conception
of the a priori as having objective validity logically,
although its subjective validity was only empirical; and
the doctrine that experience is based upon the subject
and not upon the thing, and similar forms of philosophic subjectivism. The primary experience of reality
was lacking. Sometimes this fact would suddenly dawn
upon a student of philosophy when a leading representative of the new idealism declared, in a university, for
example, that "Being" is a "value"! It would be impossible to express more shortly or more bluntly how
impossible this attitude was, and how it could only have
originated in a profound spiritual impotence. Reality
as experienced had no longer any solidity or force. It
was a lifeless shadow. And in this philosophy did but
translate into its formulas and its idiom what all felt in
one way or another. In spite of the much vaunted "real-
ism," in spite of natural science, technical achievement,
and a realist politics, man could not see the real object,
the finished article, nor even himself. He lived in an
intermediate sphere between being and nothingness,
among concepts and mechanisms among formulas and
systems, which sought to represent and control objects,
but which were not even coherent. He lived in a world
of abstract forms and symbols, which was not linked
up with the reality to which the symbols referred. We
are reminded of a wholesale manufacturer, who knows

exactly what workmen, officials, buyers, and contractors he employs, and has particulars of the whole in his register, including descriptions of all his raw materials and goods, labeled in the most accurate methods of physical-chemical research—but who knows nothing of his employees as human beings, and has no innate feeling for fine material or good work.

This attitude was also making its influence felt in the religious sphere. Nothing which was not an immediate experience or a logical datum had power to convince or was accepted without further question. The individual was sure only of that which he personally experienced, perceived, and yearned for, and on the other hand of the concepts, ideas, and postulates of his own thought. Consequently the Church was of necessity experienced not as a self-justified religious reality, but as the limiting value of the subjective; not as a living body, but as a formal institution.[2]

Religious life was thus individualistic, disintegrated, and unsocial. The individual lived for himself. "Myself and my Creator" was for many the exclusive formula. The community was not primary; it took the second place. It no longer was a natural reality which existed from the first by its own right. It had to be thought out, willed, and deliberately set up. One individual, it was believed, approached another, and went into partnership with him. But he was not from the outset bound up with a group of his fellows, the member of an organic community, sharing its common life. There was indeed no community, merely a mechanical organization, and this in the religious sphere as in every other. How little in Divine worship were the faithful aware of themselves as a community! How inwardly disintegrated the community was! How little was the individual parishioner conscious of the parish, and in how individualistic a spirit was the very sacrament of community—*Communion*—conceived!

This attitude was intensified by another factor—the rationalistic temper of the age. That alone was admitted which could be "comprehended" and "calculated." The attempt was made to substitute for the properties of things, as given in indissoluble unity of the concrete object, mathematically defined groups of relations; to replace life by chemical formulas. Instead of the soul, people talked about psychic processes. The living unity of personality was viewed as a bundle of events and activities. The age was in direct contact only with that which could be demonstrated by experiment. That something lay behind what was perceptible to the senses had first of all to be made credible by a distinct process of reflection. Already the mysterious depths of individual personality whatever moved and lived in the soul, was being questioned. And the supra-personal unity of the community was not seen at all. The community was regarded as a mere aggregate of individuals, as an organization of ends and means.

Its mysterious substance, its creative power, and the organic laws governing communal growth and development, remained inaccessible.

All this naturally exerted its influence upon men's conception of the Church. She appeared above all as a legal institution for religious purposes. There was no perception of the mystical element in her, everything in fact which lies behind her palpable aims and visible institutions, and is expressed by the concept of the kingdom of God, the mystical Body of Christ.

———◆———

This entire attitude, however, is now undergoing a profound change. New forces are at work busy in those mysterious depths of human nature where the intellectual and spiritual movements which now shape the life of a human culture receive their origin and direction. We are conscious of reality as a primary fact. It is no longer something dubious from which it is advisable to retreat upon the logical validity which seems more solid and more secure. Reality is as solid, indeed more solid, because prior, richer, and more comprehensive. Proofs are accumulating that people are willing to accept concrete reality as the one self-evident fact, and to base abstract truth upon it. We need not be astonished at this new *nominalism*. The consciousness of reality has burst upon mankind which the force of a new and a personal experience. Our age is literally rediscovering that things exist, and moreover with an individuality incalculable, because creative and original. The concrete, in its boundless fullness, is being once more experienced, and the happiness of being able to venture oneself to it and enter into it. It is experienced as freedom and wealth—I am real, and so also is this thing which confronts me in its self-determined abundance! And thought is a living relation between myself and it—perhaps, who knows, also between it and myself? Action is a real communication with it. Life is a real self-development, a progress among things, a communion with realities, a mutual give and take. That extreme critical aloofness which was formerly considered the acme of rationality is becoming more and more incomprehensible to us, a stupefying dream, which imprisoned man in an empty, dead world of concepts, cut off from the luxuriant life of the real world. Modern idealism—against which the assaults of logic were so long delivered in vain, because the foundation of the system was not proof, but a dogmatic foundation of the mental attitude of the entire age—no longer needs to be refuted. The bottom has fallen out of it. Its spell is broken, and we ask ourselves how it is that we endured it so long. A great awakening to reality is in progress.

And it is an awakening, moreover, to metaphysical reality. I do not believe that any man who is not tenaciously persisting, is not clinging to an attitude adopted long before, any man who is living in the age or even in advance of it, any longer seriously doubts the reality of the soul. Already there has been talk of a "world of spiritual objects"; that is to say, the psychic is experienced as sufficiently real to necessitate our acceptance of an entire order of being beyond the sensible. The more difficult task for the scientist is now to make the transition from the former denial, which had become a scientific article of faith, to the inevitable admission of the self-evident fact that the soul exists. And the existence of God is equally self-evident. Spiritualism and anthroposophy—in themselves so unsatisfactory—prove how powerful the consciousness of metaphysical reality has already become. In the face of such movements we find ourselves obliged to defend the pure spirituality of God and of the soul, while upholding the reality in their own order of empirical objects. And the revival of a Platonic type of thought points in the same direction. Spiritual forms are again viewed as metaphysical forces, and no longer as merely involved in the logical structure of consciousness. And many other signs of the same tendency could be adduced.

Community is admitted just as directly. The attitude of withdrawal into the barred fortress of self no longer passes, as it did twenty years ago, for the only noble attitude. On the contrary, it is regarded as unjustifiable, barren, and impotent. Just as powerful as the experience that things exist and the world exists is the experience that human beings exist. Indeed, the latter is by far more powerful, because it affects us more closely. There are human beings like myself. Each one is akin to me, but each one is also a separate world of his own, of unique value. And from this realization springs the passionate conviction that we all belong one to another, are all brothers. It is now taken as self-evident that the individual is a member of the community. The latter does not originate through one man attaching himself to another, or renouncing part of his independence. The community is just as primary a fact as individual existence. And the task of building up the community is just as primary and fundamental as that of perfecting personality.

And this consciousness of interdependence assures a most significant expression; it develops into the consciousness of nationality. "The people" does not mean the masses, or the uncultured, or the "primitives," whose mental and spiritual life, and whose system of facts and values are as yet undeveloped. All these uses of the term derive from the ideas of liberalism, the *Aufklärung*, and individualism. An entirely new note is now being sounded; something essential is being born. "The people" is the primary association of those human beings who by race, country, and historical antecedents share the same life and destiny. The people is a human society which maintains an unbroken continuity with the roots of nature and life, and obeys their intrinsic laws. The people contains—not numerically or quantitatively, but in essential quality—the whole of mankind, in all its human variety of ages, sexes, temperament, mental and physical condition; to which we must add the sum total of its work and spheres of production as determined by class and vocation. The people is mankind in its radical comprehensiveness. And a man is of "the people" if he embraces, so to speak, this whole within himself. His opposite number is the "cultured" man. He is not the people, developed and intellectualized, but a malformation, a one-sided, debased, and uprooted being. He is a product of humanism, and above all of the *Aufklarung*. He is a human type which has cut itself adrift from the ties which make man's physical and mental life organic. He has fallen away on the one hand into a world of abstraction, on the other into the purely physical sphere; from union with nature into the purely scholastic and artificial; from the community into isolation. His deepest longing should be to become once more one of the people; not indeed by romantic attempts to conform with popular ideas and customs, but by a renewal of his inmost spirit by a progressive return to a simple and complete life. The Youth movement is an attempt in this direction.

And already a new reality is beginning to appear above the horizon. Here also the use of the word needs to be purified. It need not denote the rationalist conception of "humanity," but the living unity of

11

the human race, of blood, destiny, responsibility, and labor; that solidarity which is postulated by the dogma of original sin and vicarious redemption, mysteries which no rationalist can understand.

The individual self is conscious of enrichment not only by the experience of real things, but also by the community, which expands its self-consciousness into a consciousness of a communal self. By direct sympathy, what belongs to another becomes mine, and what belongs to me becomes his.

The fully-formed community owes its existence to a combination between the awareness of objective reality and the communal consciousness. Law, justice, and the order of society are seen to be the forms by which the community exists and operates and maintains the ground of its stability. They are not limitations of life, but its presuppositions. They do not petrify it, but give it force and enable it to energize. They, of course, in turn, must be really genuinely alive. And profound changes will occur in the social structure, legal changes for example, as soon as the realization becomes more general that a matured national community needs not an individualistic but a communal system of public law; not a system of abstract principles existing merely upon paper, but a system shaped by the vital growth of the community; that its constitution cannot be the product of abstract reasoning but must grow out of the real being and life of this people.[3]

In like manner the stream of life has burst its dams. Side by side with reason and on an equal footing with it stand the will, creative power, and feeling. Being is given equal—indeed greater—importance with doing. Development and growth rank with or above action; personality whose very reality was once called in question is accepted as the most obvious or familiar object of experience. Its incomprehensibility is a datum as primary as the logical comprehensibility of its abstract concept. And the problem to be solved is that of the relations between concept and intuition, theory and experience, being and action, form and life; the way in which one depends for its existence upon the other, and unity is achieved by the conjunction of all these factors.

This life is also stirring in our consciousness of the community. We are as immediately and acutely conscious of the communal life bearing us on its current, of those creative depths from which the being and work of the community arise, as we are of the form it assumes and the logic that form expresses. A biology and, moreover, an ontology of the community are being disclosed—laws of its physical and mental nature, its organic rhythm and the vital conditions which determine its growth, usages and culture; the essential significance of its moral phenomena; the nature of such institutions as the family, the township, the state, law and property.

ROMANO GUARDINI

———— ◆ ————

Those revolutionary changes must necessarily have their repercussions in the religious community. The reality of things, the reality of the soul, and the reality of God confront us with a new impressiveness. The religious life alike in its object, content, and development is reality; the relation between the living soul and the living God, a real life directed towards Him. It is neither mere emotion nor mere theory; it is imitation, obedience, receiving and giving.[4] In the Youth movement in which the springs of the new age must be sought, the fundamental question is no longer "Does God exist?" but "What is He like? Where shall I find Him? How do I stand towards Him? How can I reach Him?" It is not "Should we pray?" but "How should we pray?" not "Is asceticism necessary?" but "What kind of asceticism?"

In this religious relation our fellow men have a vital part. The religious community exists. Nor is it a collection of self-contained individuals, but the reality which comprehends individuals—the Church. She embraces the people; she embraces mankind. She draws even things, indeed the whole world, into herself. Thus the Church is regaining that cosmic spaciousness which was hers during the early centuries and the Middle Ages. The conception of the Church as the *Corpus Christi mysticum*, which is developed in the Epistles of St. Paul to the Ephesians and Colossians, is acquiring a

14

wholly new power. Under Christ the Head the Church gathers together "all which is in Heaven, on earth, and under the earth." In the Church everything—angels, men, and things—are linked with God. In her the great regeneration is already beginning for which the entire creation "groans and is in travail."

This unity is not a chaotic experience; it is no mere outburst of emotion. We are concerned with a community formed and fashioned by dogma, canon law, and ritual. It is not merely a society, but a religious community; not a religious movement, but the very life of the Church; not a spiritual romanticism, but her existence.

This consciousness of the community is, however, caught up and permeated by the consciousness of a supernatural life. As in the sphere of natural psychology "life," which is at once so mysterious, yet so completely evident, is everywhere finding recognition, so it is in the supernatural sphere. Grace is real life; religious activity is the development of a higher vitality; the community is participation in a common life, and all forms are forms of life.

And if in the natural sphere we have acquired a clear vision for the structural laws and the organic purpose of life; if we have discovered how one thing fits another and where man's intellectual objectives lie; if consciousness of the organic is everywhere awakened, the same thing is occurring here. The profound formulas of theology once more reveal their inexhaustible significance for the spiritual life of every day. Our life, whether the life of the individual, or the life of the Church, is "in Christ, through the Holy Spirit, to the Father." The Father is the Goal, and to Him the great and final Object, is focused the vision which alone gives our religion a fixed aim.[5] He is the sublimest and all-embracing sovereign power, and the wisdom which pervades the world, the sublimity which lifts us from narrow ways. The Son is the Way, as He Himself has told us. By His Word, by His life, and by His whole Being He reveals the Father and leads us to Him: "No man comes to the Father but by me." He who acknowledges Christ, he who "sees" Him, "sees the Father also." In proportion as we become one with Christ we approach the Father more closely. And the Holy Spirit, the Spirit of Jesus, is the Leader, and shows us the way. He bestows Christ's grace, teaches Christ's truth, and makes Christ's ordinances operative. This is the law governing the organization of Christian life—the law of the Blessed Trinity. Only where order is, God is. The Father has sent the Son, and He has sent the Holy Spirit from the Father. In the Church we become one with the Holy Spirit; He unites us with the Son, "and he will surely take of his own and give to us." And in Christ we come back to the Father.

An event of tremendous importance has happened.

The religious life no longer rises solely in the self, but at the same time at the opposite pole, in the objective and already formed community. There also life originates and is thus a reciprocal movement between these two poles. It is once more what of its very nature it should be, a phenomenon of tension, an arc of flame. And it is full and free only when its process is an arc rising from two extremities. The objective is no longer merely the boundary of the subject to which religion in the strict sense is confined. It is an essential factor of the religious life, given from the very outset. It is the presupposition and content of religion.

The religious life is being released from its fatal confinement within the subject, and draws into itself the entire fullness of objective reality. As once in the Middle Ages, all things are re-entering the religious sphere, and moreover with a religious coloring and as religious values. The rest of mankind and the things of this world once more are invested with a religious atmosphere and a profound religious significance. As a result, the feeling for symbolism is coming back; concrete objects once more become the vehicles and expressions of spiritual reality. We understand how every department of a real world could find a place in the cathedrals of the Middle Ages, in its *Summas*, universal histories, encyclopedias, and cycles of legend, and moreover not as an incongruous accessory, not as an allegory stuck on from without, but filled with religious content and itself invested with a spiritual character. Many signs point towards the re-emergence of a religious world. This, however, is the Church, which gathers together under one head "what is in heaven, on the earth, and under the earth." The moment seems near for a genuine religious art, which will not be content to depict religious subjects with an unconsecrated brush, but will see the whole world spiritually as a vast kingdom of realities, comprising good and evil powers,[6] and in which the Kingdom of God is taken by storm.

All this, however, can be summed up in one word— "the Church." That stupendous fact that is the Church is once more becoming a living reality, and we understand that she truly is the One and the All. We dimly guess something of the passion with which great saints clung to her and fought for her. In the past their words may sometimes have sounded empty phrases. But now a light is breaking! The thinker, with rapture of spirit, will perceive in the Church the ultimate and vast synthesis of all realities. The artist, with a force that moves his heart to the depths, will experience in the Church the overwhelming transformation, the exquisite refinement, and the sublime transfiguration of all reality by a sovereign radiance and beauty. The man of moral endeavor will see in her the fullness of living perfection, in which all man's capacities are awakened and sanctified in Christ; the power which contrasts uncompromisingly *yea* and *nay*, and demands a decision between them; the determined fight for God's Kingdom against evil. To the politician—forget the ugliness which is usually implied by the term; it can bear a noble sense—she is revealed as that supreme order in which every living thing finds its fulfillment and realizes the entire significance of its individual being. It achieves this in relation to beings and the whole, and precisely in virtue of its unique individual quality combines with its fellows to build up the great *Civitas*, in which every force and individual peculiarity are alive, but at the same time are disciplined by the vast cosmic order which comes from God, the Three in One. To the man of social temper she offers the experience of an unreserved sharing, in which all belongs to all, and all are one in God, so completely that it would be impossible to conceive a profounder unity.

All this, however, must not be confined to books and speech, but must be put with effect where the Church touches the individual most closely—in the parish. If the process known as the "Church movement" makes progress, it is bound to lead to a renewal of parochial consciousness. This is the appointed way in which the Church must become an object of personal experience. The measure of the individual's true—not merely verbal—loyalty to the Church lies in the extent to which he lives with her, knows that he is jointly responsible for her, and works for her. And conversely the various manifestations of parish life must in turn be such that the individual is able to behave in this way. Hitherto parish life itself has been deeply tainted by that individualistic spirit of which we have spoken above. How, indeed, could it have been otherwise?

And confirmation is the sacrament by which the Christian comes into full relation with the Church. By Baptism he becomes a member of the Church, but by Confirmation he becomes one of her citizens, and receives the commission and the power to take to himself the fullness of the Church's life, and himself to exercise—in the degree and manner compatible with his position as a layman—the "royal priesthood of the holy people."

It is in the light of what has already been said that we can understand the liturgical movement. This is a particular powerful current and one more exceptionally visible from outside than within the "Church movement"; indeed, it is the latter in its contemplative aspect. Through it the Church enters the life of prayer as a religious reality and the life of the individual becomes an integral part of the life of the Church.

Here the individual is as one of the people, not a member of an esoteric group of artists and writers, as, for instance, in the books of J. K. Huysmans, but essentially one of the people. That is to say, he is comprised in the unity which finds room at the same time for the average man and the most extraordinary possibilities of heroism, the unity which comprises both the surface and the deepest roots of humanity, hard, everyday common sense and profound mysticism, which can even include crude popular beliefs which verge on superstition, and which is nevertheless alone competent to judge the realities of life and of the Church because it alone really faces life—its possibilities of development hampered in innumerable respects by poverty and narrow surroundings, and yet, as a whole, the sole complete humanity. The liturgy is essentially not the religion of the cultured, but the religion of the people. If the people are rightly instructed, and the liturgy properly carried out, they display a simple and profound understanding of it. For the people do not analyze concepts, but contemplate. The people possess that inner integrity of being which corresponds perfectly with the symbolism of the liturgical language, imagery, action, and ornaments. The cultured man has first of all to accustom himself to this attitude; but to the people it has always been inconceivable that religion should express itself by abstract ideas and logical developments, and not by being and action, by imagery and ritual.

The liturgy is throughout reality. It is this which distinguishes it from all purely intellectual or emotional piety, from rationalism and religious romanticism. In it man is confronted with physical realities—men, things, ceremonies, ornaments—and with metaphysical realities—a real Christ, real grace. The liturgy is not merely thought, nor is it merely emotion; it is first and foremost development, growth, ripening, being. The liturgy is a process of fulfillment, a growth to maturity. The whole of nature must be evoked by the liturgy, and as the liturgy seized by grace must take hold of it all, refine and glorify it in the likeness of Christ, through the all-embracing and ardent love of the Holy Spirit for the glory of the Father, whose sovereign Majesty draws all things to Itself.

Thus the liturgy embraces everything in existence, angels, men, and things; all the content and events of life; in short, the whole of reality. And natural reality is here made subject to supernatural; created reality related to the uncreated.

This full reality is shaped by the constructive laws of the Church—by dogma, the law of truth; by ritual, the law of worship; and by canon law, the law of order.

The growth itself does not take place according to a program or regulations carefully thought out, but as all life grows—rhythmically. But we cannot develop this point further now. What proportion and equilibrium are in spatial construction, rhythm is in sequence—systematic repetition in change, so that the following step repeats the previous one, but at the same time goes beyond it. In this way life grows to its fullness and the transformation of the soul is accomplished. The liturgy is a unique rhythm. Incalculable discoveries still await us in this field. What the Middle Ages experienced as a matter of course, what is already contained in the Church's rubrics, but which has vanished from the consciousness of religious people, must be rediscovered.

Its substance, however, is the life of Christ. What He was and did lives again as mystical reality. His life, infused into those rhythms and symbols, is renewed in the changing seasons of the Church's year, and in the perpetual identity of *sacrifice* and *sacrament*. This process is the organic law by which the believer grows "unto the measure of the age of the fullness of Christ." Living by the liturgy does not mean the cultivation of literary tastes and fancies, but self-subjection to the order established by the Holy Spirit Himself; it means being led by the rule and love of the Holy Spirit to a life in Christ and in Him for the Father.

We have yet to realize what constant discipline, what a profound fashioning, and training of the inner life, this demands. When we do, no one will any longer regard the liturgy as a mere aestheticism.

Creation as a whole embraced in the relation with God established by prayer; the fullness of nature, evoked and transfigured by the fullness of grace, organized by the organic law of the Triune God, and steadily growing according to a rhythm perfectly simple yet infinitely rich; the vessel and expression of the life of

Christ and the Christian—this is the liturgy. The liturgy is creation, redeemed and at prayer, because it is the Church at prayer. At Pentecost, when the fullness of the Spirit came upon the Apostles, all those tongues were not sufficient to declare the "wonderful works of God."

It often seems as though a breath from that mighty tempest is stirring in our own time! Our religion rises before us as a shape so majestic that it leaves us breathless.

But why do I speak of religion? Did the primitive Christians or the Middle Ages talk about "religion" as we use the word? Is there such a thing as "religion" for the Catholic? He is a child of the living God, and a member of the living Church.

Notes

1. This and the remarks which follow are intended merely to describe how people felt and what consciousness was theirs. It is not concerned with the essence and significance of the Church herself.

2. Naturally much in this individualism is necessary and true. These criticisms are directed solely against a false one-sidedness which impoverishes human life; against subjectivism, not against the subjective. This will be obvious from all that follows.

3. At this point the real meaning of politics becomes clear. It is no technique of deceit, lying, and violence. But it means the noble art which accepts all the concrete phenomena of life, races, classes, and without violating their distinctive characters finds room for all, but in such a fashion that their combined life and functions build up a powerful and richly endowed society. Here moral and educational problems intervene which, to the best of my knowledge, hardly anyone with the exception of F. W. Foerster has seriously tackled.

4. The constant repetition of the idea of "realization" in the writings of John Henry Newman, who experienced the individualistic crisis so intensely, is most significant. By this he means the transforming of an object from a purely verbal and conceptual entity into an experience, in which it is apprehended as a reality. This will in turn make our lives serious.

5. Because this had been widely forgotten, it was possible for Adolf von Harnack to present the message of the Father in so one-sided a manner as the content of the work of Christ, that it became, so to speak, colored with Protestantism. Every page of the Breviary, every prayer of the Mass loudly proclaims that the aim and aspiration of our whole life is directed to the Father.

6. For belief in that which is opposed to God is also religious. Only coldness and intellectual pride are irreligious. He who believes in the devil as a reality by so doing believes in God also.

25

II. The Church and Personality

If the first lecture has fulfilled its object, it has displayed the spiritual environment in which the Church appears before us today. We have seen how as the Church grows in strength a process develops which embraces our entire spiritual life. And now we have to inquire, what is the meaning of this Church, which rises before us in such majesty?

This is the object which we must keep in view. We shall not attempt to prove that the Church is true; we shall take belief in her divinity for granted. But when a scientific investigator has established the existence, in a given part of the body, of a particular organ, formed in a particular manner, he proceeds to investigate its significance for the life of the organism. In the same way we shall seek to discover what is the Church's significance for the religious life as a whole. This is the sense of our question. We shall, it is true, considerably limit the scope of our question. For we shall leave out of account the primary and deepest meaning of the Church, which is that she is God's spiritual universe, His self-revelation and the manifestation of His glory. We shall consider only its other aspect. This concerns the Church in her relation to man's existence and salvation, and her significance for the men who are her members. But we must make a further restriction. We must leave mankind out of account and concentrate wholly upon personality. That is to say, we shall inquire what is the Church's significance for the personal being and life of the man who makes his membership a living reality, for whom the Church is his very life.

———◆◆———

What is the Church? She is the Kingdom of God in mankind. The Kingdom of God—it is the epitome of Christianity. All that Christ was, all that He taught, did, created, and suffered, is contained in these words—He has established the Kingdom of God. The Kingdom of God means that the Creator takes possession of His creature, penetrates it with His light; He fills its will and heart with His own burning love and the root of its being with His own divine peace, and He molds the entire spirit by the creative power which imposes a new form upon it. The Kingdom of God means that God draws His creature to Himself, and makes it capable of receiving His own fullness; and that He bestows upon it the longing and the power to possess Him. It means—alas, the words are blunted by repetition and our hearts are so dull, or they would catch fire at the thought—that the boundless fecundity of the divine Love seizes the creature and brings it to that second birth whereby it shares God's own nature and lives with a new life which springs from Himself. In that rebirth the Father makes it His child in Christ Jesus through the Holy Spirit.

This union of man with God is God's Kingdom. In it man belongs to His Creator, and his Creator belongs to Him. Much more of profound significance could be said about this mystery, but we must be content with these few words.

This elevation of the creature is not a natural event but God's free act. It is bound up with the historical personality of Jesus of Nazareth, and with the work which He accomplished at a particular period of history. Nor is it a natural process, but an operation of Grace, exceeding all the forces of nature.

Let us examine it more closely. From the standpoint of God, it is something quite simple. But in the creature it develops to its maturity according to the forms and laws which God has established in the Spirit of man.

God's Kingdom resides in mankind. God takes possession of mankind as such, of the unity, welded by all the biological, geographical, cultural, and social ties which bind one human being to others; that mysterious unity which, though composed entirely of individuals, is more than their sum total. If this whole is to be laid hold upon by God, it is not necessary that all men should be numerically included in it. It is sufficient that God's grace should take hold of the community as such, that something which transcends the individual. This, however, can be accomplished in a small representative group. The little flock at Pentecost was already "mankind," because it was an objective community, of which the individual was a member; it was in a condition to expand, until it slowly included everything, as the mustard seed becomes the tree in which "the birds of the air...dwell." That is to say we are concerned with a line of force, the direction along which the divine action operates. God takes possession of men, insofar as a man reaches out above his natural grasp; inasmuch as men belong to a supra-personal unity, and are, or are capable of becoming, members of a community.

Insofar, therefore, as God's remodeling and uplifting power is directed towards the community as such, the Church comes into being. The Church is the Kingdom in its supra-personal aspect; the human community, reborn into God's Kingdom. The individual is "the Church," insofar as the aim of his life is to assist the building up of the community, and he is a member, a cell of it. This, however, is the case insofar as he is employing those capacities of his being which have a more than merely individual reference and are ordained to the service of the whole, which work for it, give to it, and receive from it. The Church is the supra-personal, objective aspect of the Kingdom of God—although of course she consists of individual persons.[1]

The Kingdom of God, however, has a subjective side as well. That is the individual soul, as God's grace takes possession of it in that private and unique individuality by which it exists for itself. The Church embraces a man as he reaches out beyond himself to his fellows, capable and desirous of forming in conjunction with them a community of which he and they are members. The individual personality, however, is also based upon itself, like a globe which revolves around its own axis. And as such, also God's grace takes possession of it. By this I do not mean that there exists in human beings a sphere which lies outside the Church. That would be too superficial a notion. It is truer to say that the whole man is in the Church, with all that he is. Even in his most individual aspect he is her member, although only insofar as this individuality and its powers are directed to the community. His whole being belongs to it; it is in its social reference—his individuality as related to his fellows and incorporated in the community. But the same individuality has an opposite pole. His powers are also directed inwards to build up a world in which

31

he is alone with himself. In this aspect also he is the subject of God's grace.[2]

For God is the God of mankind as a whole. As such He is concerned with the supra-personal, the community, and its members jointly find in Him the social Deity of which human society has need. But He is also the God of each individual. This is indeed the supreme and fullest revelation of His life—that for each individual He is "his God." He is the unique response to the unique need of every individual; possessed by each in the unique manner which his unique personality requires; belonging to him, as to no other besides, in his unique nature. This is God's Kingdom in the soul, Christian personality.[3]

Clearly this Christian personality is not a sphere lying outside the Church, or something opposed to her, but her organic opposite pole, demanded by her very nature, and yet at the same time determined by her.[4]

We have contrasted the Kingdom of God as the Church with the Kingdom of God as personality. We were obliged to do so, in order to grasp clearly the distinctions between them. But the question at once arises, what is the relation between them?

We must reply at once and as emphatically as possible: they are not two things separable from each other; not two "Kingdoms." They are aspects of the same basic reality of the Christian life, the same fundamental mystery of grace. There is only one Kingdom of

God; only one divine possession of man by the Father, in Christ, through the Holy Spirit. But it develops along the two fundamental lines of all organic development. And it manifests itself in accordance with the two fundamental modes of human nature—in man as he is self-contained and asserts himself as an individual, and in man as he merges in the community which transcends his individuality.

The Kingdom of God is at once the Church and individual personality, and it is both *a priori* and of its very essence. It is definitively the Church; for the Church is the transfiguration of man's nature by grace, so far as he is within the community. It is a kingdom of individual personality in every believer. It is thus both the Church and the individual Christian. They are not independent spheres. Neither can be separated from the other, even if each can be considered separately. On the contrary, of their nature and *a priori* they are interrelated and interdependent.

For the nature of the community as Catholicism understands and realizes it is not such that individual personality has to struggle for self-preservation against it. It is not a power which violates personal individuality, as Communism does, or any other variety of the totalitarian state. On the contrary, Catholic community presupposes from the outset and requires the free individual personalities as its components. In particular the Church is a community of beings, which are not simply members and instruments of the whole, but at the same time are microcosms revolving on their own axes, that is, individual personalities. Mere individuals can constitute only herds or human ant-heaps; community is a mutual relationship of personalities. This is an ethical requirement, for morality demands a free intercourse. It also results from the very structure of being, for it is only when units with their individual centers, their own *modus operandi* and a life of their own, come together, that there can arise that unity, unique in its tension and flexibility, stable, yet rich in intrinsic possibilities of development, which is termed a community.

And Christian personality is not so constituted that it is only as an afterthought associated with others to form a community. Its membership of the community does not originate in a concession made by one individual to another. It is not the case that individuals by nature independent of one another conclude a contract, by which each sacrifices a part of his independence, that by this concession he may save as much of it as possible. That is the view of society held by individualism. Personality as Catholicism understands it, looks in every direction, and thus a priori and of its very nature is social, and man's entire being enters into society. A mere sum total of individuals can produce only a crowd. If a large number join together merely by a contract for some definite object, the sole bond which constitutes their society will be this common purpose. <u>A genuine community on the contrary cannot</u> <u>be formed in this way by individuals. It exists from the</u> <u>outset, and is a supra-individual reality, however hard</u> <u>it may be to comprehend from an intellectual concep-</u> <u>tion of its nature.</u>

It is this which fundamentally distinguishes the relationship between the community and the individual as Catholicism understands it from all one-sided conceptions of it, such as Communism and the totalitarian state on the one hand, and individualism or even anarchy on the other. It is not based upon a one-sided psychology or a mental construction, but on reality in its fullness. The Catholic's conception of personality differs from every type of individualism essentially and not merely in degree. For the same individual who is a self-centered unit is at the same time conscious in his whole being, he is a member of the community, in this case of the Church. And in the same way the community is not a mere feeble social restriction or state bondage, but something fundamentally different. It differs as does living being with its innumerable aspects from an artificial construction without flesh and blood. For the community realizes that it is made up of individuals; each one of which constitutes a self-contained world and possesses a unique character. This is a fundamental truth which it is most important to understand thoroughly. Unless it is grasped, the Catholic view of the Church, indeed of society as such, must be unintelligible. We must not get our sociological principles either from Communism, state socialism, or individualism. For all these tear the living whole to pieces to exaggerate one portion of it. All are false and diseased. The Catholic conception of society and of individual personality, on the contrary, starts— like all Catholic teaching—not from isolated axioms or one-sided psychological presuppositions, but from the integrity of real life apprehended without prejudice. In virtue of his nature man is both an individual person and a member of a society. Nor do these two aspects of his being simply co-exist. On the contrary, society exists already as a living seed in man's individuality, and the latter in turn is necessarily presupposed by society as its foundation, though without prejudice to the relative independence of both these two primary forms of human life.

From this point of view also the Catholic type of humanity is reappearing at the present day, and shaking off at last the spell of State worship on the one hand, of a disintegrating self-sufficiency on the other. Here, too, we are again handling realities instead of words, and we recognize organic relationships instead of being dominated by abstract conceptions. It is for us to decide whether we shall allow ourselves to be re-enslaved or remain conscious of our mission to be true to the fundamental nature of humanity and express it freely and faithfully in word and deed.

The Church, then, is a society essentially bound up with individual personality; and the individual life of the Christian is of its very nature related to the community. Both together are required for the perfect realization of the Kingdom of God. An electric current is impossible without its two poles. And the one pole cannot exist, or even be conceived, without the other. In the same way the great fundamental Christian reality, the Kingdom of God, is impossible, except as comprising both Church and individual personality, each with its well-defined and distinctive nature, but essentially related to the other. There would be no church if its members were not at the same time mental microcosms, each self-subsistent and alone with God. There would be no Christian personality, if it did not at the same time form part of the community, as its living member. The soul elevated by grace is not something anterior to the Church, as individuals originally isolated formed an alliance. Those who hold this view have failed completely to grasp the essence of Catholic personality. Nor does the Church absorb the individual, so that his personality can be realized only when he wrenches himself free from her. Those who think this do not know what the Church is. When I affirm the "Church," I am at the same time affirming individual "personality," and when I speak of the interior life of the Christian, I imply the life of the Christian community.

37

Even now, however, the mutual relationship has not been fully stated. Both the Church and individual personality are necessary. Both, moreover, exist from the first; for neither can be traced back to the other. And if anyone should attempt to ask which of the two is the more valuable in the sight of God, he would see at once that it is a question which cannot be asked. For Christ died for the Church, that He might make her, by His Blood, "a glorious Church, not having spot or wrinkle." But He also died for every individual soul. The state in its human weakness sacrifices the individual to the society; God does not. The Church and the individual personality—both, then, are equally primordial, equally essential, equally valuable. Yet there is a profound difference between these two expressions of the Kingdom of God. Priority of rank belongs to the Church. She has authority over the individual. He is subordinated to her: his will to hers, his judgment to hers, and his interests to hers. The Church is invested with the majesty of God, and is the visible representative in face of the individual and the sum total of individuals. She possesses—within the limits imposed by her own nature and the nature of individual personality—the power which God possesses over the creature; she is authority. And, however aware the individual may be of his direct relation to God, and as God's child know that he is emancipated from "tutors and governors," and that he enjoys personal communion with

God, he is notwithstanding subject to the Church as to God. "He that hears you, hears me." "Whatsoever thou shalt bind upon earth, shall be bound also in heaven."

It is a profound paradox which nevertheless is alone in harmony with the nature of life, and, as soon as the mind's eye is focused steadily upon it, self-evident.

———◆◆———

From all this one fact emerges. The personal life of the Christian is engaged to its profoundest depth in the Church and affected by her condition. And conversely the Church is to an incalculable degree affected by the spiritual condition of her members. What concerns the Church concerns me. You see at once what this implies. It does not simply mean that a child, for instance, will be badly taught if the servant of the Church who has charge of his education is inadequate to the task. On the contrary, between the individual and the Church there is an organic solidarity of the most intimate kind. The same Kingdom of God lives in the Church and in the individual Catholic. The state of each is correlative, as the surface of the water is determined by the pipes which supply it. The individual can as little dissociate himself from the state of the Church—it would be the illusion of individualism—as the individual cell can dissociate itself from the state of health of the whole body. And conversely it is of a matter of incalculable

concern for the Church whether the faithful are men
and women of strong and valuable personality, character. The Church could never aim at a power, strength,
and depth to be achieved at the expense of the individual personality of her members. For she would
imperil the power, strength and depth of her own life.
This must not be misunderstood. The Church does
not depend for her existence and essential nature upon
the spiritual and moral condition of individuals. For,
were this the case, she would not be an objective reality. And everything said hitherto has insisted upon
her essential objectivity. But in the concrete the abundance and development of her life do depend in every
age upon the extent to which her individual members
have become what God intended them to be, developed personalities, each unique, with a unique vocation and unique capacities to be fulfilled. The relation
between the Church and the individual should never
be understood as though either could develop at the
expense of the other. This misconception is at the root
of the un-Catholic attitude to this question, whether in
its Protestant or Byzantine form.

We are Catholic insofar as we grasp—or rather, for
this is insufficient—insofar as we live the fact, indeed
feel it as obvious in our very bones as something to
be taken for granted, that the purity, greatness, and
strength of individual personality and of the Church
rise and fall together.

You now realize, I am sure, how very far short of this Catholic frame of mind our ideas are, and even more our deepest and most immediate feelings; how far the contemporary tension between the community and the individual has affected our view of the relation between the Church and the individual, thereby imperiling its very essence.

We are conscious of a tension between the Church and the individual personality, and the most enthusiastic speeches cannot abolish it. And it is not the tension of which we have already spoken, the tension inherent in the nature of their relationship, which is a source of health and life, but an unnatural and destructive tension. In the Middle Ages, the objective reality of the Church, like that of society in general, was directly experienced. The individual had been integrated in the social organism in which he freely developed his distinctive personality. At the Renaissance the individual attained a critical self-consciousness, and asserted his own independence at the expense of the objective community. By so doing, however, he gradually lost sight of his profound dependence upon the entire social organism. Consequently, the modern man's consciousness of his own personality is no longer healthy, no longer organically bound up with the conscious life of the community. It has overshot the mark, and detached itself from its organic context. The individual cannot

41

help feeling the Church to be, with her claim to authority, a power hostile to himself. But no hatred pierces deeper than that between complementary forms of life, from which we may form some idea of what this tension involves.

It will be the mission of the coming age once more to envisage truly the relation between the Church and the individual. If this is to be achieved, our conceptions of society and individual personality must once more be adequate. And self-consciousness and the sense of organic life must again be brought into harmony, and the inherent interdependence of the Church and the individual must again be accepted as a self-evident truth. Every age has its special task. And this is equally true of the development of the religious life. To see how the Church and the individual personality are mutually bound together; how they live the one by the other; and how in this mutual relationship we must seek the justification of ecclesiastical authority, and to make this insight once more an integral part of our life and consciousness is the fundamental achievement to which our age is called.

If, however, we wish to succeed in this task, we must free ourselves from the partial philosophies of the age such as individualism, state socialism, or Communism. Once more we must be wholeheartedly Catholic. Our thought and feeling must be determined by the essential nature of the Catholic position, must proceed from that direct insight into the center of reality which is the privilege of the genuine Catholic.

Individual personality starves in a frigid isolation if it is cut off from the living community, and the Church must necessarily be intolerable to those who fail to see in her the pre-condition of their most individual and personal life; who view her only as a power which confronts them and which, far from having any share in their most intimate, vital purpose, actually threatens or represses it. Man's living will cannot accept a Church so conceived. He must either rise in revolt against her, or else submit to her as the costly price of salvation. But the man whose eyes have been opened to the meaning of the Church experiences a great and liberating joy. For he sees that she is the living presupposition of his own personal existence, the essential path to his own perfection. And he is aware of profound solidarity between his personal being and the Church; how the one lives by the other and how the life of the one is the strength of the other.

That we can love the Church is at once the supreme grace which may be ours today, and the grace which we need most. Men and women of the present generation cannot love the Church merely because they were born of Catholic parents. We are too conscious of our individual personality. Just as little can that love be produced by the intoxication of oratory and mass meetings. It is not only in the sphere of civil life that such drugs have lost their efficacy. Nor can vague sentiments give us that love; our generation is too honest for that. One thing only can avail—a clear insight into the nature and significance of the Church. We must realize that, as Christians, our personality is achieved in proportion as we are more closely incorporated into the Church, and as the Church lives in us. When we address her, we say with deep understanding not "thou" but "I."

If I have really grasped these truths, I shall no longer regard the Church as a spiritual police force, but blood of my own blood, the life of whose abundance I live. I shall see her as the all-embracing Kingdom of my God, and His Kingdom in my soul as her living counterpart. Then will she be my Mother and my Queen, the Bride of Christ. Then I can love her! And only then can I find peace!

We shall not be at peace with the Church until we have reached the point at which we can love her. Not until then.

May these lectures help a little towards this consummation. But I must make one request: Do not weigh words! A particular word or proposition may well be distorted, and even erroneous. It is not my purpose to offer you nicely calculated formulas, but something deeper—*trust*. You are, I hope, listening to the underlying meaning I wish to convey, and that in the light of the whole you will correct for yourselves any verbal deficiencies or misstatements. In short you will, I am sure, make of these lectures what all speech and hearing, all writing and reading should be—a joint intellectual creation.

1. We must, however, bear in mind the following qualification. What we have said refers solely to that aspect of the Church with which sociology can deal. What the Church is—her actual essence—can never be conducted *a priori*. There is no such thing as a philosophy of the Church if it is understood to mean more than the consideration of those social phenomena to be found in her, which are also to be found in natural communities, and which reappear in the Church simply because she is a community of human beings. But in the Church these very phenomena differ from their counterparts in all other societies. Even in her natural aspect the Church is unique. And her essence, her distinctively supernatural character is exclusively the effect of a positive work of God, of the historical personality of Christ and her historical institution through Him. Only from revelation can we learn what the Church is in her essence. We can never do more than describe her as that community of faith and grace which Christ founded, and which continues to live on in history as the Catholic Church, with her distinctive and unique character. Only on this presupposition are such books as Pilgram's *Physiologie der Kirche* or André's *Kirche als Keimzelle der Weltvergöttlichung* valuable—indeed, of very considerable value.

2. This is not a contradiction, but a contrast. One term of a contradiction precludes the other—good and bad, yes and no, for example, exclude each other. Every living thing, however, is a unity of contrasts which are differentiated from each other, yet postulate each other. The firm, yet flexible, simple, yet creative, unity of the living organism can only be grasped intellectually as a web of contrasts. I hope to explain this point thoroughly in another book.

3. This word is not a good one. It is colored by the associations of individualism, the doctrine of individual autonomy, and above all of pure ritualism. St. Paul certainly would not have talked about "personality." The notion of Christian personality is as different from its philosophic counterpart as the notion of the "Church," Christ's Church, differs from that of the "religious society." However, I know of no better word; I use it, therefore, in the sense in which Our Lord speaks of a "child of God," and St. Paul, in his Epistles, of the individual Christian as distinct from the community.

46

4. This personal sphere has been detached from the religious life as a whole by Protestantism and every other individualistic system and developed in a one-sided manner. Thus the direct communication between God and the redeemed, who is, however, at the same time a member of the Church, was perverted into the autonomy of a completely independent and self-sufficient personality. And the healthy tension of the relationship established by the very nature of its terms was replaced by an unnatural constraint.

III. The Way to Become Human

We propose to consider the meaning of the Church. I have already attempted to sketch it in general outline. For the individual the Church is the living presupposition of his personal perfection. She is the way to personality.[1]

Before, however, we go into details, allow me to make a preliminary observation. When I tried to explain the Church's significance for individual personality, objections, perhaps, came into your minds. Your inner glance saw many defects confronting it. Your thoughts traveled back to many personal disillusionments, and therefore you possibly felt that what I said was untrue. You thought that what I said was indeed true of the ideal, of a spiritual church, but that the actual Church is not, and does not accomplish, what I was maintaining. I owe you an answer to this objection.

Those who could speak of the meaning of the Church must also speak of her defects. Even the Church cannot escape the tragedy inherent in all things human, which arises from the fact that infinite values are bound up with what is human and consequently imperfect. Truth is bound up with human understanding and teaching; the ideal of perfection with its human presentation; the law and form of the community with their human realization; grace, and even God Himself—remember the Sacrifice of the Mass—bound up with actions performed by men. The Infinitely Perfect blends with the finite and imperfect. This, if we dare say it, is the tragedy of the Eternal Himself, for He must submit Himself to all this if He is to enter the sphere of humanity. And it is the tragedy of man, for he is obliged to accept these human defects, if he would attain the Eternal. All this is as applicable to the Church, as to every institution that exists among human beings. But in her case it has an additional poignancy.

For the highest values are here involved. There is a hierarchy of values, and the higher the value in question, the more painfully will this tragic factor be felt. Here, however, we are concerned with *holiness*, with God's grace and truth, with God Himself. And we are concerned with man's destiny which depends on this divine reality—the salvation of his soul. That the State should be well ordered is, of course, of great importance, and so is a well-constructed system of the natural sciences; but in the last resort we can dispense with both. But the values bound up with the Church are as indispensable on the spiritual plane as food in the physical order. Life itself depends upon them. My salvation depends upon God; and I cannot dispense with that. If, however, these supreme values, and consequently the salvation of my soul, are thus intimately bound up with human defects, it will affect me very differently from, for instance, the wrecking of a sound political constitution through party selfishness.

But there is a further consideration. Religion stands in a unique relation to life. When we look more closely, we see that it is itself life; indeed, it is fundamentally nothing but that abundant life bestowed by God. Its effect, therefore, is to arouse all vital forces and manifestations. As the sun makes plants spring up, so religion awakens life. Within its sphere everything, whether good or bad, is at the highest tension. Goodness is glorified, but evil intensified, if the will does not overcome it. The love of power is oppressive in every sphere, but in the religious most of all. Avarice is always destructive, but when it is found in conjunction with religious values or in a religious context, its effect is peculiarly disastrous. And when sensuality invades religion, it becomes more stifling than anywhere else. If all this is true, the human tragedy is intensified in religion, since any shortcoming is here a heavier burden and more painfully felt.

Yet a further point. In other human institutions the realization of spiritual values is less rigid. They leave men free to accept or refuse a particular embodiment. The value represented by a well-ordered political system, for instance, is indeed bound up with particular concrete states. But every man is free to abandon any given state and to attach himself to another, whenever he has serious grounds for taking the step. In the Church, however, we must acknowledge not simply the religious value in the abstract, nor the mere fact that it is closely knit with the human element, but that it is bound up with this, and only this particular historic community. The concrete Church, as the embodiment of the religious value demands our allegiance. And even so, we have not said enough. The truth of Christianity does not consist of abstract tenets and values, which are "attached to the Church." The Truth on which my salvation depends is a Fact, a concrete reality. Christ and the Church are that truth. He said: "I am the truth." The Church, however, is His Body. But if the Church is herself Christ, mystically living on; herself the concrete life of truth and the fullness of salvation wrought by the God-man; and if the values of salvation cannot be detached from her and sought elsewhere, but are once and for all embodied in her as an historical reality, the tragedy will be correspondingly painful, that this dispenser of salvation is so intimately conjoined with human shortcomings.

Therefore, just because the Church is concerned with the supreme values, with the salvation of the soul, because religion focuses the forces of life and thus fosters everything human, both good and bad, because we are here confronted with an historical reality which as such binds us and claims our allegiance, the tragedy of the Church is so intense. So intense is it that we can understand that profound sadness which broods over great spirits. It is the *tristezza così perenne* ["this persistent sadness"]. which is never dispelled on earth, for its source is never dry. Indeed, the purer the soul, the clearer its vision, and the greater its love for the Church, the more profound will that sorrow be.

This tragedy is an integral part of the Church's nature, rooted in her very essence, because "the Church" means that God has entered human history; that Christ, in His nature, power, and truth, continues to live in her with a mystical life. It will cease only in Heaven, when the Church militant has become the Church glorified. And even there? What are we to say of the fact that a particular man who should have become a saint and who could have attained the full possession of God, has not done so? And who will dare to say that he has fully realized all he might have been? We are confronted here by one of those ultimate enigmas before which human thought is impotent. Nothing remains but to turn to a power which is bound by no limits, and whose creative might "calls those things that are not, as those that are"—the Divine Love. Perhaps the tragedy of mankind will prove the opportunity for that love to effect an inconceivable victory in which all human shortcomings will be swallowed up. It has already made it possible for us to call Adam's fault "blessed." That the love of God exceeds all bounds and surpasses all justice is the substance of our Christian hope. But for this very reason what we have already said remains true.

To be a Catholic, however, is to accept the Church as she is, together with her tragedy. For the Catholic Christian this acceptance follows from his fundamental assent to the whole of reality. He cannot withdraw into the sphere of pure ideas, feelings, and personal experience. Then, indeed, no "compromises" would be any longer required. But the real world would be left to itself, that is, far from God. He may have to bear the reproach that he has fettered the pure Christianity of the Gospel in human power and secular organization, that he has turned it into a legal religion on the Roman model, a religion of earthly ambitions, has lowered its loftiest standards addressed to a spiritual elite to the capacity of the average man, or however the same charge may be expressed. In fact, he has simply been faithful to the stern duty imposed by the real world. He has preferred to renounce a beautiful romanticism of ideals, noble principles, and beautiful experiences rather than forget the purpose of Christ—to win reality, with all that the word implies, for the Kingdom of God.

Paradoxical as it may seem, imperfection belongs to the very essence of the Church on earth, the Church as an historical fact. And we may not appeal from the visible Church to the ideal of the Church. We may certainly measure her actual state by what she should become, and may do our best to remove her imperfections. The priest is indeed bound to this task by his ordination, the layman by Confirmation. But we must always accept the real Church as she actually is, place ourselves within her, and make her our starting point.

This, of course, presupposes that we have the courage to endure a state of permanent dissatisfaction. The more deeply a man realizes what God is, the loftier his vision of Christ and His Kingdom, the more keenly will he suffer from the imperfection of the Church. That is the profound sorrow which lives in the souls of all great Christians, beneath all the joyousness of a child of God. But the Catholic must not shirk it. There is no place for a Church of aesthetes, an artificial construction of philosophers, or congregation of the millennium. Man needs a Church that is a church of human beings; divine, certainly, but including everything that goes to make up humanity, spirit and flesh, *earth*. For "the Word was made Flesh," and the Church is simply Christ, living on, as the content and form of the society He founded. We have, however, the promise that the wheat will never be choked by the tares.

Christ lives on in the Church, but Christ crucified. One might almost venture to suggest that the defects of the Church are His cross. The entire Being of the mystical Christ—His truth, His holiness, His grace, and His adorable person—are nailed to them, as once His physical body to the wood of the Cross. And he who will have Christ must take His cross as well. We cannot separate Him from it.

I have already pointed out that we shall only have the right attitude towards the Church's imperfections when we grasp their purpose. It is perhaps this—they are permitted to crucify our faith, so that we may sincerely seek God and our salvation, not ourselves. And that is the reason why they are present in every age. There are those indeed who tell us that the Early Church was ideal. Read the sixth chapter of the Acts of the Apostles. Our Lord had scarcely ascended to Heaven when dissension broke out in the primitive community. And why? The converts from paganism thought that the Jewish Christians received a larger share than they in the distribution of food and money. This surely was a shocking state of affairs? In the community through which the floods of the Spirit still flowed from the Pentecostal outpouring? But everything recorded in Holy Scripture is recorded for a purpose. What should we become if human frailties actually disappeared from the Church? We should probably become proud, selfish, and arrogant; aesthetes and reformers of the world. Our belief would no longer spring from the only right motives, to find God and secure eternal happiness for our souls. Instead, we should be Catholics to build up a culture, to enjoy a sublime spirituality, to lead a life full of intellectual beauty. The defects of the Church make any such thing impossible. They are the Cross. They purify our faith.

Moreover, such an attitude is at bottom the only constructive type of criticism, because it is based on affirmation. The man who desires to improve a human being must begin by appreciating him. This preliminary acknowledgment will arouse all his capacities of good and their operation will transform his faults from within. Negative criticism, on the contrary, is content to point out defects. It thus of necessity becomes unjust and puts the person blamed on the defensive. His self-respect and justifiable self-defense ally themselves with his faults and throw their mantle over them. If, however, we begin by accepting the man as a whole and emphasize the good in him, all his capacities of goodness, called forth by love, will be aroused and he will endeavor to become worthy of our approval. The seed has been sown, and a living growth begun which cannot be stayed.

We must, therefore, love the Church as she is. Only so do we truly love her. He alone genuinely loves his friend who loves him as he is, even when he condemns his faults and tries to reform them. In the same way we must accept the Church as she is, and maintain this attitude in everyday life. To be sure we must not let our vision of her failings become obscured, least of all by the artificial enthusiasm aroused by public meetings or newspaper articles. But we must always see through and beyond these defects her essential nature. We must be convinced of her indestructibility and at the same time resolved to do everything that lies in our power, each in his own way and to the extent of his responsibility, to bring her closer to her ideal. This is the Catholic attitude towards the Church.

My introduction has been lengthy. But it was important; so important indeed that I believe that what follows will seem true to you, only in proportion to your agreement with what has been said hitherto.

We saw in the last lecture that the problem we have to face is not the alternative of "the Church or the individual?" It concerns rather the relation between these two realities. In theory our aim must be a harmony between the two in which of course the precedence of the Church is fully safeguarded. But the intellectual and spiritual current of a period always flows in a particular direction. Harmonious syntheses are achieved only in brief periods of transition between two different epochs, for example when an age whose outlook is extremely objective and in which the social sense is powerfully developed is yielding to an epoch of individualism. Soon, however, one tendency predominates, and moreover, that which is opposite to the former. The Catholic attitude does not preclude the emphasis being laid on one aspect, otherwise it would be condemned to a monotonous uniformity and would deprive man of history. It demands only that the other aspect shall not be rejected, and coherence with the whole be preserved. That is to say, a particular aspect brought into prominence by the historical situation is emphasized, but is at the same time brought into a vital and organic relationship with the whole. A door is left open to the particular disposition of the historical present, but it is attached to the whole, which always in a sense transcends history. This whole is less actual, but in return it partakes of eternity. It is less progressive, but instead wise, and in the depths is alone in accordance with reality.

Our age is in process of passing from the individualistic and subjective to the social and objective. A stronger emphasis will therefore be laid on the Church. And these lectures will do the same. They will inquire how individual personality, by surrender to the Church, becomes what it should be. My lecture today will show how the Church is the way to individual personality. And I shall proceed from the fact that the Church is the spiritual locality where the individual finds himself face to face with the Absolute; the power that effects and maintains this confrontation.

ROMANO GUARDINI

Let us try to realize how deeply we are sunk in relativism, that is, the attitude of mind which either denies an Absolute altogether, or at any rate tries to restrict it within the narrowest limits.

We have lived through the collapse of an edifice which we expected to endure for an incalculable period of time, the collapse of the political structure of our country and its power, of the social and economic order existing hitherto, and with it of much besides. We can watch the social sense changing. And our mental attitude towards objects and life in general is equally changing. These changes go too deep to be dismissed with a few words. Artistic vision has changed; the expressionism, which had gradually become familiar, is already yielding, and the desire is springing up for a new classicism. A scientific and philosophical view of the universe is forming, which strives to attain a loftier and a freer understanding of objects in accordance with their essential nature.

Faced with these profound changes we become rather more acutely conscious of what in truth is always happening—that the attitude of the soul towards itself, its environment, and the first principles of being, is continually shifting. The forms of human life, economic, social, technical, artistic and intellectual, are seen to be in a state of steady, if slight, transformation.

We live in a perpetual flux. As long as this flux is not too clearly perceived, as long as a naive conviction ensures a strong underlying reserve of vitality, or deeply rooted religious beliefs balance the increase of knowledge, life can endure it.

But in periods of transition, and when centuries of criticism have worn away all fixed belief, the flux forces itself on the mind with an evidence from which there is no escape. The condition ensues which ten years ago was universally predominant, and is still widespread today; a sense of transience and limitation takes possession of the soul. It realizes with horror how all things are in flux, are passing away. Nothing any longer stands firm. Everything can be viewed from a thousand different angles. What had seemed secure disintegrates, on closer inspection, into a series of probabilities. To every thing produced there are many possible alternatives. Every institution might equally well have been ordered otherwise. Every valuation is only provisional.

Man thus becomes uncertain and vacillating. His judgments are no longer steady, his valuations unhesitating. He is no longer capable of action based on firm conviction and certain of its aim. He is at the mercy of the fashions prevalent in his surroundings, the fluctuations of public opinion, and his own moods. He no longer possesses any dignity. His life drifts. He lacks everything which we mean by character. Such a man is no longer capable of conquest. He cannot overcome error by truth, evil and weakness by moral strength, the stupidity and inconstancy of the masses by great ideas and responsible leadership, or the flux of time by works born of the determination to embody the eternal values.

But this spiritual and intellectual poverty is accompanied by a colossal pride. Man is morbidly uncertain and morbidly arrogant. The nations are confused by pride, parties are blinded by self-seeking, and rich and poor alike are the prey of an ignoble greed. Every social class deifies itself. Art, science, technology—every separate department of life considers itself the sum and substance of reality. There is despairing weakness, hopeless instability, a melancholy consciousness of being at the mercy of a blind irrational force—and side by side with these a pride, as horrible as it is absurd, of money, knowledge, power, and ability.

Impotence and pride, helplessness and arrogance, weakness and violence—do you realize how by the continued action of these vices true humanity has been lost? We are witnessing a caricature of humanity. In what then does humanity in the deepest sense of the term consist? To be truly human is to be conscious of human weakness, but confident that it can be overcome. It is to be humble, but assured. It is to realize man's transience, but aspire to the eternal. It is to be a prisoner of time, but a freeman of eternity. It is to be aware of one's powers, of one's limitations, but to be resolved to accomplish deeds of everlasting worth.

What is a complete humanity? When neither of these two essential aspects is obscured, but each is asserted and developed; when they neither destroy each other nor drive each other to extremes, but blend in an evident unity replete with inner tension yet firm, imperiled, yet assured, limited, yet bound on an infinite voyage, this is a complete humanity, And a man is human insofar as he lives, consciously, willingly, and with a cheerful promptitude as a finite being in the midst of time, change, and the countless shapes of life— but at the same time strives to overcome all this flux and limitation in the eternity, and infinity, which transfigure them. A man is human insofar as he truly and humbly combines these two essential aspects. Herein lies the inexpressible charm of all things human—a mystery pregnant with pain and strength, desire and confident hope.

———◆◆———

Well then—the Church is always confronting man with the Reality which creates in him the right attitude of mind: namely, the Absolute.

She confronts him with the Unconditioned. In that encounter he realizes that he himself is dependent at every point, but there awakens in him the yearning for a life free from the countless dependencies of life on earth, an existence inwardly full. She confronts him with the Eternal, he realizes that he is transitory, but

destined to life without end. She confronts him with
Infinity, and he realizes that he is limited to the very
depths of his being, but that the Infinite alone can
satisfy him.

The Church continually arouses in him that
tension which constitutes the very foundation of his
nature: the tension between being and the desire to be,
between actuality and a task to be accomplished. And
she resolves it for him by the mystery of his likeness
to God and of God's love, which bestows of its fullness that which totally surpasses the nature. He is not
God, but a creature, yet he is God's image and therefore capable of apprehending and possessing God.
Capax Dei, as St. Augustine says, able to grasp and hold
the Absolute. And God Himself is love. He has made
the creature in His own image. It is His will that this
resemblance should be perfected by obedience, discipline, and union with Himself. He has redeemed man,
and by grace has given him a new birth and made him
god-like. But all this means that God has made man for
His living kingdom.

But observe this encounter with the Absolute, in
which man faces the Infinite and sees clearly what he
is, and what It is; but which at the same time awakens
the longing for this Absolute Godhead and the confident expectation of its fulfillment by His love—this
fundamental experience of Christianity, truth, humility, yearning love, and confident hope in one, is the

moment in which for the first time in the spiritual sense man becomes truly human.

This transformation of a creature into man in the presence of the Absolute is the work of the Church.

———◆◆———

She accomplishes it in various ways. In the first place, through her very existence, through that character which Jesus compared to a rock, the living self-revelation of the eternal God in her.

But in particular there are three essential expressions of the Absolute in the Church—her dogma, her moral and social system, and her liturgy.

The thought of modern man is relativist. He sees that historical fact is at every point conditioned by something other than itself, and everything, therefore, appears subject to change. Experimental research has made him extremely cautious, and he is wary of drawing conclusions. He has become accustomed to critical thinking, and does not readily venture beyond hypotheses and qualified statements. Statistics have taught him conscientious regard for exactitude, and he is apt to demand of any conclusion a complete experimental proof which is unattainable. He has thus become uncertain and hesitant where truth is concerned.

At this point the Church comforts him with dogma. We shall not discuss its detailed content. We are solely concerned with the fact that we are here presented with and apprehend truths unconditionally valid, independently of changing historical conditions, the accuracy of experimental research, and the scruples of methodical criticism. Nor shall we consider the factor of Catholic doctrine which is itself temporally conditioned and therefore changeable. We are dealing only with its unchangeable content, with dogma in the strict sense. He who approaches dogma in the attitude of faith will find in it the Absolute. He thus comes to realize how extremely unreliable is his own knowledge. But he is confronted by Truth divinely guaranteed and unconditional. If he honestly assents to it, he becomes "human."

He has a correct valuation of himself. His judgments are clear, free, and humble. But at the same time he is aware that there is an Absolute, and that it confronts him here and now in its plenitude. By his faith he receives the Absolute into his soul. Humility and confidence, sincerity and trust unite to constitute the fundamental disposition of a thought adequate with the nature of things. Henceforward the unconditional organizes the believer's thought and his entire spiritual life. Man is aware of something, which is absolutely fixed. This becomes the axis upon which his entire mental world turns, a solid core of truth which gives consistency and order to his entire experience. For it becomes the instinctive measure of all his thinking even in the secular sphere, the point of departure for all his intellectual activity. Order is established in his inner life. Those distinctions are grasped without which no intellectual life is possible—the distinction between certainty and uncertainty, truth and error, the great and the petty. The soul becomes calm and joyful, able to acknowledge its limitations yet strive after infinity, to see its dependence, yet overcome it.

This is what is meant by becoming human.

Moral purpose is relative; ideals of perfection, standards of goodness, and codes of individual and of social behavior are fluctuating and unstable. Effort is thus crippled, and the will, powerless when important decisions must be made, will in compensation give a free rein to arbitrary impulse in some particular sphere.

The Church confronts man with a world of absolute values, an essential pattern of unconditional perfection, an order of life whose features bear the stamp of truth. It is the Person of Christ. It is the structure of values and standards which He personified and taught, and which lives on in the moral and hierarchical order of the Church.

The effect thus produced is the same, as before, though now in the field of valuations and moral judgment, in the life of practice and production; man is confronted with what is unconditionally valid. He faces and acknowledges his own essential limitation. But at the same time he sees that he can attach his finite life at every point to God's infinite life, and fill it with an unlimited content. He there finds rest. He rejoices in the fact that he is a creature, and still more that he is called to be a "partaker of the divine nature." His inner life becomes real, concentrated around a fixed center, supported by eternal laws. His goal becomes clear, his action resolute, his whole life ordered and coherent—he becomes human.

Men envisage their relationship with God in various and shifting fashions. One man beholds God in every object, in tree and stone and sea. To another He speaks from the rigid and sublime laws of thought and duty. A third sees Him as the Great Organizer and Architect. Yet another finds Him in the life of the community, in love and in neighborly assistance. One man has a clear conception of God; for another He is a vague entity, the Great Incomprehensible; to a third He is an abstraction. Indeed, the same man may have different conceptions of God according to his age, experience, or moods. The danger thus arises that man may make God in his own image, and so form a finite and petty conception of Him; that his longing and prayer may no more reach out freely beyond himself, but may degenerate into a dialogue with an enlargement of his own portrait.

In the liturgy the Church displays God as He really is, clearly and unmistakably, in all His greatness, and sets us in His presence as His creatures. She teaches us those aboriginal methods of communion with God which are adapted to His nature and ours—prayer, sacrifice, sacraments. Through sacred actions and readings she awakes in us those great fundamental emotions of adoration, gratitude, penitence and petition. In the liturgy man stands before God as He really is, in an attitude of prayer which acknowledges that man is a creature and gives honor to God. This brings the entire spiritual world into the right perspective. Everything is called by the right name and assumes its real form—face to face with the true God, man becomes truly man.

———— ✦ ————

That man should see with perfect clearness what he is a creature; but that he should rejoice in this fact, and regard it as the starting point of his ascent to the Divine, that he should be humble, but strive after the highest; sincere, but full of confidence, and so for the first time be truly human—this is the work of the Church. She tells man everywhere, "You are but a creature, yet made in God's image, and God is Love. Therefore He will be yours, if only you will it."

ROMANO GUARDINI

Notes

1. The way, that is an indispensable, but not exclusive way. The more resolutely an individual acknowledges himself for what he is, and at the same time endeavors to become and to work out that which God has destined for him by his individual nature, the more powerfully can the Church affect him and complete the personality to which she can raise him. It must once more be repeated that the individualists imagine a contradiction in this an "alternative," where there is in reality the indispensable pre-condition of organic change. The more unreservedly I live in the Church, the more completely I shall become that which I ought to be. I can, however, live in the Church as God, and she herself require it, only to the degree in which I mature, awaken to my natural vocation, and became a self-realizing personality. There is a mutual reciprocity of cause and effect.

IV. The Road to Freedom

When the Catholic Christian handles a vital issue theoretically or practically, the situation should be immediately altered. It should be as when something is brought out from a false light into the full and clear light of day; or an object previously held in the violent grasp of some boorish bully has been released from his possession and passes into the hands of one who can respect and appreciate it.

Every object brought into the Catholic sphere of influence and subjected to the Catholic spirit should recover its freedom and once more fully realize its nature. The Catholic spirit should impose the true standard, the great should appear great, and the petty, petty; and light and shadow put in the right place.... Yes, so it would be if one were really Catholic! Then indeed we should possess that true Goodness which sees all things as they are, and brings freedom. And life, which everywhere is suffering violence, would again breathe freely in all that we are and do, and all things be made new!

This is certainly expected of the Catholic Christian by those who are looking on at him from without. They do not expect him to talk brilliantly, or to live in an exceptional fashion remote from life, arbitrary and one-sided. There is an intelligentsia which in an intellectual fashion does violence to life more brilliantly and more significantly than he. These onlookers do not expect this from the Catholic. They expect him to possess something of Adam's pure vision, and that creative power with which the first man named all things according to their nature. They expect to find in him a glance which proceeds from the center of the soul and penetrates the heart of objects, and to which they reveal themselves completely; that great love which redeems the silent misery of the world.[1]

But we are not really Catholic, if the term is to be understood in its full and exacting implication, and it is our great, if painful, good fortune that we realize how little we are Catholic. But to be truly Catholic is the real, indeed the only genuine form of human existence, its way of life dictated at once by man's deepest nature and by divine revelation. It is a way of looking at things and of thinking about them which becomes instinctive. This, however, can be formed only in the operation of a long tradition, when the personal attitude of individuals has taken shape in objective forms, customs, organizations, practical achievements, and these exert a formative influence upon individuals, to be in turn remolded by them. The Reformation and the *Aufklärung* have wrought incalculable destruction; we are all under the influence of the individualistic, naturalistic, and liberal spirit.

We are, therefore, no doubt taking a risk when we speak about human life, without being really Catholic. But we to it tentatively, and well aware that the greatest merit we can achieve is to be forerunners. Our master is St. John the Baptist, who said that after him One was to come Whom the Holy Spirit would baptize with fire. It is only after us that there will come those who will think, feel, produce and speak, out of the fullness of Catholic life. Ours must be the meager joy of being allowed to prepare their way.

———————

We are going to speak about one of the supreme treasures of life—about freedom.

How shop-soiled this word has become, and yet it is one of the most noble! How often have we Catholics allowed the most intimate of our possessions to be taken from us; and filled with the spirit of error, and then listen suspiciously to what our soul should utter with the deep accents of her native speech!

Freedom—what a dubious connotation the word has acquired! Yet it contains the sum of what Christ has brought us. It is one of those royal words with which the spiritual masters of the Middle Ages described the majesty of God. "God the free," they called Him.

———————

What then is freedom? What sort of man, exactly, is the free man?

To answer that freedom is the absence of external constraint, the power to choose, according to one's own will, among several possible courses, gives no notion of the wealth comprised in the term. For it cannot be contained in a short phrase.

Let us try to bring to light something of this treasure. Each one of us possesses a pattern of his being, the divine idea, in which the Creator contemplated him. It comprises not only the universal idea of human nature, but everything besides, which constitutes this particular individual. Every individual is unique, and a unique variety of human nature. Indeed, the Rembrandt-German[2] could say truly, could even maintain, strictly speaking, that a number of people should not be counted together, because in reality each is unique, and cannot be compared with the rest.

When this unique quality of a man's individual being is allowed to emerge, and determines all his existence and activities; when he lives from the center of his own being, not, however, putting an artificial restraint upon himself, but naturally and as a matter of course, he is a free man. He is free who lives in complete harmony with the divine idea of his personality, and who is what his Creator willed him to be. He has achieved a complete equilibrium, the effect of a tension but a resolved tension, a powerful yet gentle rhythm of life, a life at once rich and concentrated, full yet restrained.

All this, however, is but a part of true freedom. The free man must also see things as they are, with a vision not clouded by mistrust, nor narrowed by prejudice, nor distorted by passion, whether hatred, pride, or selfishness; must see them in the fullness of their objective reality, and in their genuine measure. He must see them in their entirety, rounded off, displayed on all sides, in their true relations with other objects, and in their right order. He will thus see them from the standpoint of their divine idea, just as they are. His glance will pierce from the center of his soul to the center of its objects. His love, issuing from an entire heart, will embrace their entire fullness. And his action, supported by a personality not divided against itself, grasps the world steadily and draws from it that which had awaited the hand of God's child, to be brought pure and complete into the light.

That man should respond to the true nature of things with the integrity of his own nature and in the unique fashion of his divinely ordained individuality, that the divine idea within and that without encounter each other in his personal life—this is freedom.

But freedom is even more than this. A man is free when he can see the great as great and the small as small; the worthless as worthless and the valuable as valuable; when he views correctly the distinctions between different objects and different conditions; the relations between objects and their measure. He is free when he recognizes honestly the hierarchy of objects, and their values, placing its base and its apex, and each intermediate point in its right position. He is free when he apprehends the idea in its purity, but contemplates in its light the complete reality; when he sees everyday life with all its rough and tumble and all its shortcomings, but also what is eternal in it. He is free when his vision of the idea does not blind him to reality, and everyday existence does not make him oblivious of the idea, when he "can gaze upon the stars, but find his way through the streets."

To see all this, to hold fast to the vision with stout heart and unswerving will, and act in accordance with it amid the confusion of appearances and passions—this is freedom.

But he must do this not because a compulsion is upon him, but because he himself is resolved upon it;

not merely as the laborious and painful application of principles, but because the impulse and volition of his own nature impel him, and because the very heart of his personality is thereby fulfilled—thus and not otherwise is he free.

Freedom is a great thing—the supreme fulfillment and the purest standard of worth, truth, and peace.

And with all that we have said we still have not plumbed the ultimate depth of freedom. It is that the man who is truly free is open to God and plunged in Him. This is freedom for God and in God.

You will ask, if that is freedom, are we free? Outwardly, of course, we are often free. We can resist a palpable restraint. Psychologically also, for we can choose between right and left. But freedom in the comprehensive sense which we have given? No, we must certainly acknowledge that we are slaves.

Here once more we encounter the mission of the Church—she, and she alone, conducts us to this freedom.

———— ◆◆ ————

What are the bonds which a man must break to win this complete freedom?

There are in the first place those external circumstances which impede a man's development. These can be very strong; but if his energy is sufficient, he will in the end overcome them, either outwardly, by altering them, or inwardly, by a free renunciation which raises him above them.

The intellectual environment binds more potently, through current opinions, customs and tradition; through all those imponderable but constantly operative forces of example and of influence, mental and emotional. These things penetrate to the profoundest depths of the spirit. Even genius cannot wholly break their spells. And we average people are all subject to these influences, whether we consent to them or oppose them.

Just consider for a moment the extent of their sway. What cannot be effected by a slogan if the environment is favorable? No one can altogether escape its power. How powerful are the intellectual tendencies of an epoch! So potent can they be that ideas which are simply incomprehensible when the intellectual situation has changed may receive the unquestioning credence due to dogmas of faith. Do we not ask ourselves with amazement today how certain ideas of Kant's could have been accepted as so many dogmas, disagreement with them regarded as a proof of intellectual weakness? Remember, too, how powerful a compulsion is exercised by highly developed forms of art if the cultural environment is congenial. Think of the manifold ways, often so subtle as to defy discovery, in which certain political, social, or economic forms, for example, democracy or capitalism, mold a man's entire psychology; how a type of humanity recognized as ideal, for example, the knight, the monk, or the traveler, shapes men by its influence to the very core of their being. Against such forces the individual is powerless.

Reflect how, under the spell of such a general tendency, a particular age, the Renaissance, for example, with the decision born of the sense of an immeasurable superiority, rejects what another age—in this case the Middle Ages—had ardently embraced, how we are only now beginning to regard the Renaissance and what followed it as a disaster, and the Middle Ages as—rightly understood—our future. And bear in mind that this was no mere change of externals, but of man's attitude to essentials, values and ideas. In view of all this we have only one choice. Either we must canonize relativism in one shape or another, whether in its cruder form, the doctrine of the milieu, or in the form given to it by Keyserling, psychologically more profound and resting on a metaphysical basis, or embrace with our whole soul a power which can emancipate us.

It is the Church.

In the Church eternity enters time. Even in the Church, it is true, there is much which is temporal. No one acquainted with her history will deny it. But the substance of her doctrine, the fundamental facts which determine the structure of her religious system and the general outlines of her moral code and her ideal of perfection, transcend time.

In the first place, of her very nature she thinks with the mind, not of any one race, but of the entire and Catholic world. She judges and lives, not by the insight of the passing moment, but by tradition. The latter, however, is the sum total of the collective experience of her past. She thus transcends local, national and temporal limitations, and those who live and think with her have a *point d'appui* above all such restricted fields of vision, and can therefore attain a freer outlook.

The Church of her nature is rooted, not in particular local conditions or particular historical periods, but in the sphere above space and time, in the eternally abiding. She enters, of course, into relation with every age. But she also opposes each. The Church is never modern. This was the case even in the Middle Ages. We have only to read between the lines of the *Imitation* to detect it. The present always reproaches the Church with belonging to the past. But this is a misconception; the truth is that the Church does not belong to time. She is inwardly detached from everything temporal, and is even somewhat skeptical in her attitude to it.

And she has also had to endure the constant charge that she is not national, that she represents foreign nations, not the particular nation in question.

It is a misconception of the truth. In the last resort she is not concerned with nations, but with humanity as a whole, and individual men and women. These, however, are the two expressions of humanity which touch eternity, while everything lying between them, and in particular political and national organizations, are bound to time.

The Church, therefore, stands amid the currents of intellectual fashion like a vast breakwater. She is the power which resists the spell of every historical movement, no matter what. She opposes the strength of her misgivings to every force which threatens to enslave the soul—economic theories, political slogans, human ideals of perfection, psychological fashions—and repudiates their claim to absolute validity. The Church is always the opponent of the contemporary. When an idea is new, it exercises a special attraction. It is fresh and novel; opens up to the mind unexplored avenues of thought, and thus arouses far more enthusiasm than its intrinsic value merits. And when a people becomes acquainted with a culture previously unknown and the conditions are favorable, it takes an irresistible hold upon that people, as Asiatic culture, for example, is affecting us today. In the same way new tendencies in art, new political principles, indeed novelties in every sphere down to such externals as fashions of dress and the conventions of social intercourse. If the environment is receptive, everything new is doubly potent, like oxygen *in statu nascendi.* Very often its power bears hardly any proportion to its true value, with the result that our picture of it is falsified to the point of distortion. The present, therefore, is always to a certain extent a hallucination and a prison. It has always attacked the Church, because it is over-excited, and her timeless calm resists its petulant importunacy; because it is one-sided, and her comprehensiveness transcends its limited vision. And the Church has always been the foe of the present, because its unspiritual violence enslaves the soul and its obtrusive clamor drowns the voice of eternity. In every age the Church opposes what is *here* and *now* for the sake of *forever*; the contemporary tendencies and "politics," for the sake of those aspects of humanity which are open to eternity—individual personality and mankind. When this has been understood, a great deal becomes clear.

He who lives with the Church will experience at first an impatient resentment, because she is constantly bidding him to oppose the aims of his contemporaries. So long as he regards what is being said everywhere, the public opinion prevalent at the moment, as the last word on any question, and makes parties or nations his criteria of value, he will inevitably feel himself condemned to obscurantism. But once the bandage has been removed from his eyes, he will acknowledge that the Church always releases those who live in her from the tyranny of the temporal, and to measure its values gives him the standard of abiding truth. It is a remarkable fact that no one is more skeptical, more inwardly independent of "what everyone says" than the man who really lives in the Church. And as a man abandons his union with her, to the same degree does he succumb to the powerful illusions of his environment, even to the extent of sheer superstition. And surely the decision between those two attitudes involves the very roots of human culture. The Church is indeed the road to freedom.

———————

But we have not spoken so far of the strongest bonds of all, those imposed by a man's own character.

There are, in the first place, psychological characteristics common to all men as such, passions, for example, and tendencies of the will. Only if we could conceive knowledge as the purely logical operations of a purely logical subject, as a kind of intellectual mechanism, which always functions smoothly, and which can immediately be set in motion under any conditions, would it be possible to regard it as unaffected by the other psychological functions. But the subject of thought is not an abstract, logical subject, but a living man; thought is a vitally real relation between man and the object of his thought. In the function of thinking all his other activities and states participate, fatigue, for example, and energy strung to the tensest pitch, joy and depression, success and failure. The experience of every day proves that our intellectual productivity, the direction of our thoughts and the nature of our conclusions, are influenced by the vicissitudes of daily life. Our psychological states may assist, hamper, or completely prevent acts of knowledge, strengthen or weaken the persuasiveness of arguments. Desire, love, anger, a longing for revenge, gratitude—anyone who is honest with himself must admit how enormously the force of an argument, apparently purely logical, fluctuates in accordance with his prevalent mood, or the person who puts it forward. Even the climax of the cognitive process—the evidence, the subjective certainty of a judgment, a conclusion, a structure of reasoning—is to an enormous extent subject, as you can see for yourselves, to the influence of psychological states and the external environment. It is a strange chapter in practical epistemology.

So far we have been speaking only of speculative thought. There remains the whole order of values, judgments, pronouncements about good and evil, the lawful and the unlawful, the honorable and the dishonorable, the valuable, the less valuable, and the worthless. How enormously these judgments depend on the fact that the man who forms them acknowledges, esteems, and loves the value in question, or rejects, hates, and despises, and on his general attitude towards men and things; whether he is receptive or self-contained, trustful or suspicious, has keener eyes for good or evil.

When you reflect upon all this, you must admit that our thought and valuations are permeated to the depths by the influences of a man's personal characteristics, his stage of development, and his experiences.

By this I do not mean that our thought and judgments are merely a product of our internal and external conditions; no reduction of thought and valuation to psychological and sociological processes is implied. Their nucleus is intellectual, but it is embedded in those processes. Thought has an objective reference, and is always striving to realize it more purely, that is to say, to grasp more perfectly objective truth. It has an objective content, this very truth—and becomes more perfect as this content becomes richer and more distinct. In spite of this, however, thought is life, and valuation is life—a vitally real relation between man and the object. And everything which affects that man or the object plays its part in the process.

What will bring us release from this imprisonment? Most certainly no philosophy; no self-training, no culture. Man can be set free only by a power that opens his eyes to his own inner dependence and raises him above it, a power that speaks from the eternal, independent at its center of all these trammels. It must hold up unswervingly to men the ultimate truths, the final picture of perfection, and the deepest standards of value, and must not allow itself to be led astray by any passion, by any fluctuations of sentiment, or by any deceits of self-seeking.

This power is the Church. As contrasted with the individual soul she may easily give an impression of coldness and rigidity. But to the man who has grasped her essence, she becomes pure life. Certainly it is a life so abundant that the weak, irritable man of today cannot easily experience it. The Church clears the path to freedom through the trammels of environment and individual psychology. In spite of all her shortcomings, she shows man truth seen in its essence, and a pure image of perfection adapted to his nature. He is thus enabled to escape his personal bondage.

Once more we must delve deeper, and at last we shall reach our conclusion.

We have spoken of the inner pattern contained in every individual personality which determines its unique quality. The individual is not a human being in general, but bears a stamp peculiar to himself. He embodies a distinctive form in virtue of which he realizes human nature in a special way. It is the organic ideal and fundamental law of his entire being and activity. It is expressed in everything he is or does; it determines his disposition and external attitude. It is, however, the task of the individual—we shall return to this point later—to acknowledge this individual form, bring it out, see its limitations, and place it in its due relation to the world as a whole. The strength of the individual lies in this unique quality. It represents what God desires him to be, his mission and his task. But at the same time it is the source of his weakness.

Consider first those more general mental types which classify men into distinct groups, that is to say, fundamental types of character. Thought is determined by them, the way in which things are seen, will and emotion, and the attitude towards self, man, the world, and God.

We shall sketch one example of these types of character, though only in general outline. We shall call it the synthetic type. A man of this type is interested in similarity and combination. This is already evident in his own nature. There thought, will, activity, and emotion strongly tend towards unity and effect a thoroughgoing harmony. Such a man gets quickly into touch with things, and can easily pass from one to another. In objects he sees first of all their similarities, the connecting links and numerous transitions between them. He is powerfully aware of their unity, and if he gives a free rein to his native temper he will reach some type of monism, that is to say, a conception of the universe based wholly on the tendency to likeness and unity which pervades reality. He is, of course, aware of the distinctions between things, but regards them as of secondary importance and is disposed to relegate them increasingly to the background and to explain them away as mere stages of development, transitional forms, and modes of the one great unity. He will even by degrees transform the relation between God and the universe into a unity, and regard Him as simply the energy at work in all things, maintaining and animating them. And his practice will correspond with his thought. His fundamental attitude will be one of conciliation unless, indeed, as a result of the law of psychological ambivalence, he develops a passionate antagonism towards external objects, which, however, is at bottom determined by his sense of affinity with them. In every sphere he seeks a compromise. He explains evil as due to accidental imperfections, or as a necessary step in the development of good. Thus in practice and theory he is a monist, though his monism may wear a rationalist, aesthetic, or religious color.

A man of this type proves and disproves, unaware of the extent to which he is in the power of his own disposition. He persistently selects from reality those features which suit his nature, and passes over or distorts those which are opposed to it. In the last resort his entire view of the world is an attempt to establish his personal preference by rational proofs.

The opposite temper may express itself similarly. It gives birth to that fundamentally critical attitude which in any sphere notices past and present unlikenesses, what differentiates one object from another, their limitations and dividing lines. For men of this type the world is dissolved into isolated units. The distinctive qualities of objects stand out sharply side by side; the classifications made by thought are not linked up with sensation and desire. The distinctions between what is and what ought to be, between duty and right, and moral choices stand out rigid and inexorable. Conflicts, the decision between alternatives, are universal.

If this type of man follows his bent to the full, he also is enslaved. He, also, chooses, values, and measures in accordance with "his own mind," and is convinced that the result is objective truth. When the intellectual processes of a mind dominated by its period are listed in the light of their psychological presuppositions, the effect is peculiarly devastating. A host of affirmations, chains of reasoning and systems of valuations, apparently purely rational, prove but the slightly veiled expression of a particular psychological temperament. One of the most striking instances of this is Kant. His writings develop a system of thought at first sight as purely objective as could be conceived. But simultaneously they reveal their author's most intimate personality. To us, whose mentality is so utterly different, this latter aspect stands out clearly, like the original writing of a restored palimpsest, and we cannot understand how a philosophy so largely the self-expression of a genius could be mistaken for a discovery of the fundamental nature of objective reality. But unless some higher source of truth safeguards us against the danger, we shall inevitably yield credence to some other teacher who proclaims as objective truth what is but the expression of his own mentality, or formulate as serious fact, and with a great display of reasoning, matters which we have devised to express our personal attitude to life.

To return to the two types we described above—neither is free. First and foremost both are slaves as men, as human types. For there exists in every human being, side by side with his predominant mentality, its opposite. Therefore, the synthetic type of mind is also capable of criticism, and the critical type is not devoid of the power of synthesis. But in each case the complementary disposition is weaker; the mentality takes its character from the predominant tendency. But every living organism is subject to a law we may term the economy of force. It tends to use those organs which are particularly developed, so that the rest become increasingly atrophied. Each type, therefore, should develop its complementary aspect to the utmost of its power. Only by this mutual balance it will achieve complete and harmonious development. But the man who is left to himself develops one-sidedly. The predominant trait of his inner psychological composition increasingly asserts itself and thrusts the rest into the background. Over-developed in one direction he is stunted in another. Such a nature, however, is an enslaved nature, for only a being which has developed freely and harmoniously all its native capacities is free.

Moreover, a man whose development is thus one-sided is not free in relation to his environment. For of the rich abundance of its concrete reality he can see only one aspect—that aspect which is adapted to his particular temperament, and for which the powers he has specially fostered have given him a peculiarly acute vision and comprehension. He is thus held captive by it, and incapable of taking an all-round view of reality.

Such men do not live with their full nature, nor in accordance with the idea of their personality, which, whatever its particular emphasis, is always a whole, but merely with a fragment of their true selves. And their life is not in contact with objects as concrete wholes, but merely with artificial selections from them. Each, however, by a singular delusion, maintains that he is complete and his attitude the right one, his impoverished and mutilated world God's free world of full reality.

There are other types and corresponding ways of regarding the world. Each is a power, each the way to a distinctive outlook. But each is also a net liable to entangle the man who casts it. The different types mingle, and the degree of their combination varies. Their energy, warmth, and wealth vary. To these must be added national, local, and vocational characteristics, and those derived from heredity or environment. And finally, there are those enigmatic qualities which may be said to constitute the coloring, idiosyncrasy or mannerism of the individual, that wholly unique something which belongs to the one individual alone. All these blend with his fundamental type and foster its independent development.

Remember, also, that the instincts of self-preservation, self-love, and the sense of honor, feed a man's predominant disposition, that all his personal experiences are viewed in its light and adjusted to it. You will now be able to gauge its strength.

How then can a man thus in bondage to his disposition be set free?

He must acknowledge, and to the very core of his being, that reality includes all its possible aspects, is all-round. He must recognize that this reality can be grasped only by a subject equally comprehensive in his knowledge, his valuations and his activities; and that he himself does not possess this comprehensiveness, but is fragmentary, the realization of one possibility of human nature among a host of others. He must recognize the errors which this one-sidedness produces, and how they narrow the outlook and distort the judgment.

He must indeed fully accept his own special disposition, for his nature and his work are based upon it. But he must also fit it into the entire scheme of things. He must correct his own vision of the world by the knowledge of others, complete his own insights by those of other men, and thus stretch out beyond himself to the whole of reality; and this not only in his knowledge, but in his judgments of value and practical conduct.

That is to say, he must not efface his distinctive character and attempt to make his life a patchwork externally sewn together. His distinctive character must always remain the foundation. But character must become vocation, a mission to accomplish a particular work, but within an organic whole and in vital relation to it. Then one-sidedness will become fruitful distinction, bondage be replaced by a free and conscious mission, obstinate self-assertion by a steadfastness in that position within the whole which a man recognizes to be his appointed place.

Anyone who honestly attempts this task quickly realizes that he cannot accomplish it by himself. Then is the moment of decision. Will he abandon the attempt? Will he acquiesce in the impossibility? Will he become a skeptic? Or will he arrogantly endeavor to make his inner impotence tolerable by declaring it the only right attitude? In either case, he remains the slave of his own inner bonds, in the deepest sense a Philistine, however eloquent the language with which he proclaims his servitude. Or else his determination to possess truth, reality, the whole, is ready for the sacrifice which alone will lay the way open, ready "to lose his soul, in order to save it." If this is his disposition, he will experience the Church as the road to freedom.

Of her nature the Church is beyond and above these bonds, and he who "surrenders his soul to her, in her shall win it back," but free, emancipated from its original narrowness, made free of reality as a whole.

―――――◆◆――――

The Church is the whole of reality, seen, valued, and experienced by the entire man. She is co-extensive with being as a whole, and includes the great and the small, the depths and the surfaces, the sublime and the paltry, might and impotence, the extraordinary and the commonplace, harmony and discord. All its values are known, acknowledged, valued, and experienced in their degree and this not from the standpoint of any particular type or group, but of humanity as a whole.

The whole of reality, experienced and mastered by the whole of humanity—such, from our present standpoint, is the Church.

The problems with which we are faced here involve experience as a whole. No part of it may be detached from the whole. Every partial question can be correctly envisaged only from the standpoint of the whole, and the whole only in the light of a full personal experience. For this, however, a subject is required which itself is a whole, and this is the Church. She is the one living organism which is not one-sided in its essential nature. Her long history has made her the repository of the entire experience of mankind. Because she is too great to be national her life embraces the whole of humanity. In her, men of diverse races, ages, and characters think and live. Every social class, every profession, and every personal endowment contribute to her vision of the whole truth, her correct understanding of the structure of human life. All the stages of moral and religious perfection are represented in the Church up to the summits of holiness. And all this fullness of life has been molded into a tradition, has become an organic unity. Superficialities are subordinated to deeper realities; intermediate values take precedence of the trifling and the accidental. The fundamental questions of man's attitude to life have been the meditation of centuries; so that the entire domain of human experience has been covered and the solution of its problems matured. Institutions have had to be maintained through vicissitudes of period and civilization, and have reached a classical perfection. Consequently, even from the purely natural point of view, the Church represents an organic structure of knowledge, valuation, and life, of the most powerful description. To this we must add her supernatural aspect. The Holy Spirit is at work in the Church, raising her consistently above the limits of the merely human. Of Him it is said that He "searches all things." He is alone the Spirit of discipline and abundant life. To Him "all things are given."

He is enlightenment and love. He awakens love, and love alone sees things as they are. He "sets in order charity" and causes it to become truth with a clear vision of Christ and His Kingdom. He makes us "speak the truth in love." Thus the Church is sovereign above man and above the world, and can do full justice to both.

Dogma that is revealed and supernatural truth binding our assent, is the living expression of this living organism. The entire body of religious truth which it records is seen by a complete man. And it determines the attitude towards truth of the individual Catholic.

And that form of religion in which the entire man enters into a supernatural communion with God—namely, the liturgy—is another living expression of this living organism. It determines the Catholic attitude towards religion in the stricter sense.

Finally, the Church's discipline and constitution—her moral law and ideal of perfection—are yet another living expression of this organism. They determine the Catholic attitude towards ethics.

The Church holds up before man this truth, this scale of values, and this ideal of perfection; and not as merely possible or advisable, but as obligatory. She calls upon man to rise above his narrowness and grow up to this complete truth, this comprehensive ideal and universal rule of life. She commands it, and disobedience is sin. Only thus does the demand receive sufficient weight to counterbalance human selfishness, with its exaggerated and tenacious self-assertion.

If man obeys and accepts the fundamental sacrifice of self-surrender and trusts himself to the Church; if he extends his ideas to the universal scope of Catholic dogma, enriches his religious sentiment and life by the wealth of the Church's prayer, strives to bring his conduct into conformity with the lofty, complete pattern of perfection, a pattern, moreover, which molds the private life of the spirit presented by her communal life and her constitution, then he grows in freedom. He grows into the whole, without abandoning what is distinctively his own. On the contrary, for the first time he sees his individuality clearly when it is confronted with all the other human possibilities to be found in the Church. He sees its true significance to be a member of the whole. He perceives it as a vocation, a God-given task, the contribution made possible by his unique character as an individual, which he has to make towards the great common task of life and production.

Thus man develops into a personality. It is rooted in his individuality, but essentially related to the whole. It involves an individual outlook, the consequence of its uniqueness, but this individual outlook is harmonized at every point with the outlook of others because it never loses sight of the whole. It involves also a joyful determination to realize its own nature, but within the framework of the entire organism. Thus the outlook of the genuine personality is comprehensive and recognizes other men's points of view. He divines their meaning, and views his own vocation in relation to the whole. Such a man will not display instant enmity towards a personality of different type to his own, as one species of animals is hostile to another. On the contrary, he will coordinate both within the superior unity to which both belong, in the performance of a common task in which each supplements the other. He evinces that great power of acceptance which finds room for other types, and is therefore able to share their life. Thus his wealth increases, for what belongs to others is also his.

My attention has been drawn to a saying of St. Paul's in which the Christian's consciousness of this supreme freedom of his entire being finds striking expression: "The spiritual man judges all things: and he himself is judged of no man" (1 Cor. 2:15). The true Christian is sovereign. He possesses a majesty and a freedom which remove him from the jurisdiction of the unbeliever. He cannot on principle be subject to his judgment, since the unbeliever cannot focus the Christian within his field of vision. The vision of the former, on the contrary, embraces "all things," and his standard is absolute. How remote is the impoverished consciousness of our Catholicity from this attitude of St. Paul, in which perfect humility—all his Epistles reveal it—is united with the knowledge that he possesses, not one point of view among others, but the unique and absolute point of view; genuine humility combined with the sublime consciousness of absolute and perfect supremacy.

This is the meaning of *sentire cum Ecclesia*—the way from one-sidedness to completeness, from bondage to freedom, from mere individuality to personality.

Man is truly free in proportion as he is Catholic. But he is Catholic to the extent that he lives, not within the narrow confinement of his purely individual and separate existence, but in the fullness and integrity of the Church, to the extent, that is to say, that he has himself become identified with "the Church."

Notes

1. I do not think that I am exaggerating the case. What else are those numerous men and women seeking in the Church, who are looking towards her today? No doubt some may be influenced by a romantic preciosity, others, by the desire to find something solid in whatever quarter, without any genuine conviction that here, and here alone, truth is to be found; and fashion also plays its part, as in the interest in Buddhism or primitive cultures. This cannot be denied. But there is more than this. We can detect the expectation that in Catholicism the Essential—the Eternal, the Absolute—finds its due recognition. The man of today expects to find a substantial piety in the Church, independent of time, place or fashion, reality—of being and conduct—in every department of life. And it will be a bitter disappointment for which we shall all be jointly responsible, if this expectation is disappointed, not by the Church, but by her members.

2. TRANSLATOR'S NOTE: Julius Langbehn (1851–1907) became famous as a result of his book *Rembrandt als Erzieher*, published in 1890. This work is a criticism of German pre-war culture, which Langbehn viewed as heading for disaster. At the same time it sets forth his belief in the passing of the "age of paper" into a new "age of art," which was to be brought about through the primary forces inherent in the German people. Langbehn was received into the Church in 1900.

V. Community

Ideas have their seasons, as plants have their seasons of growth, flowering, and ripening of fruit. The seed is capable of growth from the beginning, but does not germinate until the spring comes. So it is with ideas. Every idea is abstractly possible at any period, but in the concrete cannot become a living growth either in the life of the individual or of society at any epoch indiscriminately. This would be possible only if thought were to be a mechanical process, the operation of an isolated reason. It is, on the contrary, a vital process of a living person, and therefore affected by the forces and states both of the individual and the community to which he belongs. An idea becomes powerful and fertile in a man only when its due season has come; when his other ideas are so ordered that it can take its place among them; when his soul gives it a vital response, and there are psychological tensions, which it relaxes or intensifies. And in society an idea becomes fruitful, takes root, and develops its intrinsic possibilities only when the soil is prepared for it.

Thus the idea—or rather the experience—of society has found its appointed hours. Only a little while ago man felt himself a self-contained microcosm. His ties with his fellow-men—the State for example, the family, affinity of ideas—he was apt to regard either as illusions or as institutions serving purely utilitarian ends or assuring his safety. The one thing of which he was certain was himself, his existence in and for himself. Of others, and of fellowship with them, he was conscious only as something dubious and shadowy.

This was due to a psychological defect. He lacked the instinctive awareness of external reality, and in particular of other minds. He was not conscious of their inner life as a datum of his own experience, at least not as something actively affecting him. This attitude could find expression in totally different ways, from icy indifference to ruthless violence. A desire, it is true, for others made itself felt, the longing to be assured that a fellow-man is indeed there, a longing for understanding and comradeship. But it was always cut short by the despairing thought, "It is impossible. I am imprisoned in my solitary isolation." A fundamental sentiment of individualism cut men from their fellows.

If man was to escape despair or weary resignation,

there remained nothing for him but to make a virtue of his dire necessity, and a very stern and bitter virtue it was. He must transform his yearning into pride, and his desire into refusal; he must attempt to convince himself that "the common life makes men common," and a proud isolation is the only noble attitude.

But when men's eyes were opened, how false all this was seen to be! They were opened, not by arguments—arguments are so weak in vital questions— but by a psychological transformation. Man became totally changed. New forces were at work in his soul, and he outgrew individualism. For his new outlook the possibility of a community has become self-evident. Nor does it arise from the deliberate conjunction of self-contained individuals. This is the erroneous conception which is impoverishing our social life and dividing the nations No society is something to be taken for granted which requires no proof. It is as primary and as necessary as individuality. And today we ask ourselves how could we have put up so long with our self-imposed isolation

Is not the present distress of Europe the last and most terrible spasm of this old disease? When the right time comes, the perception will triumph that one nation is as dependent upon the others, as one individual upon his fellows. The doctrines of the philosophy of isolation have not succeeded in keeping men apart. They possessed a shadowy existence so long as men's souls were strangers to each other. But as soon as the social sense of community awoke, all such theories were swept away. For the nations also this spring will come. Their eyes will be opened; and they will see that they belong to each other. On that day all doctrines of national selfishness, all the economic and political systems based on mistrust and mutual isolation, will vanish in smoke.

Yes, this experience of human community has come to many, and the rest have at least been influenced by it The path to the souls of others lies open. What matter to us the doctrines of individualism, subjectivism, and solipsism? Is the way to the soul of another man after all so much further than the path to my own? The spell is dissolving. The common life does not make men common. That is true only of the wrong type of community A good society is the source of happiness and power. It tests the pliability and power of resistance of our personality. It is in the highest sense a task, and a lofty enterprise.

So strong indeed has the will for community become—the word indeed, like every other valuable thing, is already deteriorating into a cheap slogan—that it is attracting men almost too powerfully to their fellows. Already we are becoming aware of the baneful possibilities of an exaggerated cult of the community. It is capable of destroying personality. We are beginning to understand the element of truth in the older individualism and to realize that society also has its problem.

The problem whether the souls of others are or are not accessible to us is not the only one. It was answered once and for all when man's fundamentally social nature was first experienced. But the answer has raised a further problem: what is the relation between the free individual and society? What kind of society is valuable, what kind the reverse? What kind of society is noble, what kind degrading? Recognizing independent personality and real community with others as the two poles of human life, we inquire, how should the one be constituted, if the other is to co-exist with it? How is the one to be made perfect by the other?

I will ask you to be patient while I tell you something about the last meeting of the Quickborn Association[1] at Burg Rothenfels. On that occasion the demands of the community were emphasized. The individual, we were told, is bound to his fellows by a natural loyalty, and is pledged to them with all he is and all he has. He must regard himself as a member of the same community with other classes and sections of his countrymen, giving to them all and receiving from them all.

Suddenly in the midst of these discussions, as though by a concerted plan, there sprang up at various points, and gathered strength, the idea of personality. The community must be so constituted that the dignity and inner freedom of the individual personality remain possible within it. For free personality is the presupposition of all true community. Those who grasped what was happening were astounded. Never before had I so profoundly experienced the power of life to maintain itself spontaneously, when it is not repressed by force.

This indeed is the supreme problem—how can a society be full-blooded and deep-rooted, a mutual surrender of its members very selves, and at the same time inherited personality continue to flourish vigorously and freely?

Once more I must repeat, it is beyond the scope of man's natural powers. One of two things must happen. Either the power of community will burst all bounds, swamp the free personality of the individual, and strip him of spiritual dignity, or else the individual personality will assert itself victoriously, and in the process sever its organic bonds with the community. So deeply has original sin shattered the fundamental structure of human life.

But the Church stands before us as the one great power which makes possible a perfect community when members are genuine personalities.

———— ◆◆ ————

First and foremost, she produces a true community. She effects a community of truth, the common possession of which is those supreme supernatural realities of which faith makes us conscious. They are the foundations of the supernatural life, for all the same—God, Christ, grace, and the work of the Holy Spirit.

What does this mean for the community? All its members stand upon the same foundation. In all alike the same forces are at work. The same aims are acknowledged by all. Their judgments are based on the same standards of valuation. They recognize the same ideals of human moral perfection, and their fundamental dispositions are identical. In spite of all their dissimilarities, how close must be the bond between men, who take their Catholic faith seriously. How deep must be the knowledge one can have of another! For he knows the motives which finally decide his moral decisions and the beliefs which guide his conduct of life.

One man can have this knowledge of another because the lives of both are rooted in the same ultimate realities. One can help another, because he no longer need find reasons for trusting him. The deepest grounds of mutual trust are evident to both. Real consolation becomes possible, because its grounds are admitted by both parties. There is a common seriousness of purpose, a common consecration, and a common worship, for the same sublime facts and mysteries are honored by all alike. There is a common endeavor and a common struggle, because the final aims of all are the same. There is a common joy—the joy of the Church's festivals—for a cause of rejoicing need not be sought far afield, and after anxious search. Joy is everywhere, and can therefore be a factor and bond of community.

There is also a community of sacrifice, a community of mutual love, of command and obedience. No one can genuinely yield interior obedience if he is not aware of an ultimate bond between himself and his superior. But when he is aware of it, trust enters into his obedience, confidence into the command. Moreover, there can be no community of love without a bond, upon which the mutual self-surrender is based. Thus the community of truth becomes a community of love, of obedience, and of command. These, however, are the forces which constitute society, also the ways in which a bridge is built between man and man, by superiority, subordination, and equal cooperation.

And all this is realized, not timidly and distrustfully, but from a professed consciousness of interdependence, by a mutual trust, and responsibility. But this is possible only when that first fundamental community of truth exists, the foundation of all other manifestations of community.

———— ♦ ————

There is a community of life, and it is immeasurably deep. The same current of grace flows through all alike, the same active power of God. The same real Christ is present in all, as the ideal and prime exemplar of perfection, our incentive to pursue it and the creative power which makes it possible.

The sacrament of community, Communion, is incomprehensible. In it man is one with God; God is personally united with him, and is given to him as his very own. But with this one God not only one man is united, but all his fellows. And each receives God into his personal being; yet each receives Him on behalf of the others also on behalf of husband or wife, of children, parents, relatives and friends—for all those to whom he is bound by ties of love.

There is a community of spirit and spiritual life— the mystical Body of Christ. Through Baptism the individual is born into it, into new, supernatural life common to all who live by it. But as yet he is merely a member of this organism. Confirmation makes him an adult member, and gives him rights, duties, and responsibilities in it. It gives him the commission and the power to pursue his calling as work for the Kingdom of God, with and for others. Holy Communion deepens his community with God, with others in God. By sin it is ruptured or impaired; in the sacrament of Penance man acknowledges his fault before the divinely appointed representative of the ecclesiastical community, makes satisfaction to it, and is received back into it. Extreme Unction gives him the strength to remain loyal to it in sickness and death. Marriage intertwines the roots of the natural community of the individual

and the race with those of the supernatural community. Finally, in Holy Orders, he who has been baptized
and confirmed receives a power to act as God's representative, command and lead. Thus the sacraments are
forms and processes, in which the life of the supernatural community begins, progresses, recovers lost
ground, and is continually propagated.

Holy Mass is throughout a communal act. This
truth has been widely forgotten. It has often been made
the private devotion of the individual. But the evidence
of the first Christian centuries proves its communal
character to the hilt. The bishop officiated, and his
priests concelebrated with him, as at the present day
newly consecrated priests concelebrate at their ordination. The people brought their gifts to the altar, and
from among these were chosen the bread and the wine
which were to be the material of the sacrifice offered
for all. And these offerings were themselves recognized
as symbols of the community. As the bread consists of
many grains of wheat, and the wine has been pressed
from a multitude of grapes, the mystical Body of Christ
consists of many individuals. The people brought their
offerings to the altar in person, that all might be drawn
into the mystical unity to be effected when the substance
of the bread and wine could be changed into the Body
and Blood of Christ. All shared in the divine banquet,
after they had banished from their hearts by the kiss
of peace everything inimical to community life. When

the sacred bread was broken, portions were taken to prisoners and the sick. One bishop would send them to another, as a sign that all were united in a community transcending the limitations of space. And after each celebration a particle of the sacred bread was preserved until the next and dipped in the chalice, to show that this unity transcended time. To discover the roots of this sentiment we must read Our Lord's discourse after the Last Supper (John 13–17), and the Epistles of St. Paul and St. John. These sources bring home to us with an overwhelming force the fact that Christ instituted His sacrifice and sacrament as communal acts, expressions of the community between God and man, and between men in God, all "in Christ," Who "has made us partakers of the divine nature." Such was the belief and practice of the Apostles, and of the Church after them. Read what the Apostolic Fathers wrote on this topic, the epistles of St. Ignatius, for instance, and then above all read the liturgy itself. And though today, this communal character of the liturgy is not clearly brought out in its details, the Holy Sacrifice, or indeed the liturgy as a whole, is intelligible only by those profoundly imbued with the communal spirit and the will to participate in the community life.

―――――◦◦―――――

Contemplate for a moment those dogmas of the Church specifically concerned with the *community*.

In the beginning we find a community of responsibility and destiny. So profound is the solidarity of mankind, that the obedience of the first man would have been the safeguard of all; and his guilt was the guilt of all. This is the mystery of original sin. It is intolerable to the individualist, who has not grasped the extent of human solidarity. But the man who has understood that every self exists also in his neighbor; that every man shares the life of all other men, and that this happiness and suffering are bound up with theirs, will realize that, in the dogma of original sin, the Church has really touched the very foundation of all human society.

But it is this very solidarity which makes the community of redemption possible. Since every man in his profoundest being is thus bound up with his fellows, so that another's guilt can become his, the atonement made by the One can be the atonement made by all the rest. God's Son becomes man, and takes upon Himself the guilt of the entire human race. This is no empty phrase, or sublime imagination. Gethsemane is sufficient proof that it was a most awful reality, a most real experience. Jesus became our representative, and His sufferings thus became the property of our race. He redeemed us, not by His example, doctrine or instructions—all these are of secondary importance—but by the representative and atoning satisfaction in which He assumed before God the responsibility of our guilt. So far reaching is this objective community of atonement, that by its power any child, without any co-operation on its part, is reborn into a new life and mode of existence.

We now come to the solidarity between the regenerate, that is, the community or Communion of Saints. The one grace of Christ flows through them all as a single stream of life. All live by the same pattern, this example which influences them all. The one Holy Spirit is at work in them all. Each possesses grace not merely for himself, but for all the rest. He passes it on in every word, every encounter with others, every good thought, and every work of charity. Every increase of the grace he possesses, by the greater fidelity, the deepening and inner growth of his spiritual life which it effects, swells the stream of grace for all the others. Whenever an individual grows in knowledge and love, the others are also affected, and not only through speech, writing, or visible example, but also directly, by an immediate and substantial transmission of love and light from soul to soul.

The prayer of my fellows, their works, their growth in grace and purity are mine also. When we encountered a pure and profound spirit—a man nearer to God than ourselves, and in whom the current of life flows fresh and strong—did we not form the wish, "I would like a share in you"? In the Communion of Saints this actually comes to pass. There is something unutterably magnificent and profound in the thought that I am to share in all the purity and fullness of supernatural life hidden in the souls of others, and it is mine, too, in the solidarity of Christ's Body.

Have you ever thought about the community of suffering? Have you considered that one man transmits to another not only the force of example, speech, and instruction, not only the superflux of grace and the efficacy of prayer and intercession, but also the power of suffering? Have you ever contemplated a truth of awe-inspiring profundity: that whenever one member offers his suffering to God for others in the community of Christ's Passion, that suffering becomes a life-giving and redeeming force for those for whom it has been offered up, and where nothing else could bring them help at any distance in space and in spite of any intervening barriers.

Not one of us knows to what extent he is living by the power of grace which flows into him through others—by the hidden prayer of the tranquil heart, the atoning sacrifices offered up by persons unknown to him, and the satisfaction made on his behalf by those who in silence offer themselves for their brethren. It is a community of the deepest and most intimate forces. They are silent, for nothing noisy can produce these substantial effects. But it cannot resist them because their source is God.

This community transcends all boundaries. It knows nothing of distance. It embraces all countries and peoples. It transcends the bounds of time, for in it the past is as active as the present. From this point, tradition, which is so often regarded in a purely external aspect, becomes a living realization. And this community transcends the boundaries of this life, for it extends beyond the grave, embracing—both the Saints in Heaven, and the souls in Purgatory.

"That they all may be one": thus Christ prayed in the hour before His Passion—one in God, and one with each other. That prayer is being continually fulfilled in the Church.

The Church is "the truth in love," as St. Paul so magnificently describes it. She is truth, in the deepest sense of living truth, essential truth; a flawless harmony of being a divine fullness of life, a living creation. But it is a fullness of truth which is love, and is constantly striving to become a greater love. It is a light, which is at the same time a glowing heat, a treasure which cannot be contained in itself but must communicate itself to others, a stream which needs must flow, a possession which must be common to all, must give itself freely to all. The Church is love. She is truth, which communicates itself. She is the treasure which must be the common property of all. She is the life, which multiplies itself, takes hold of all, and of its very nature must be a common life, a life of boundless mutual donation in which all belongs to all.

Our contemplation must here ascend to the perfection and exemplar of society, the Triune God. My best utterance here is but a stammering. But permit me to speak as best I can.

God is the pure life of truth. Its fullness, however, is so vast that it is productive, and God possesses it as the Father—that is to say, as a generating Person—and transmits it to the Son. And when in turn—I speak according to our human usage, in terms of before and after, though in reality the whole process is eternal—the Son stands before the Father as the begotten fullness of divine Truth, their mutual knowledge kindles a mutual and eternal love, and this love of Father and Son flames up as the Holy Spirit.

This community is infinite. It is an infinite life, an infinite possession, in which all things are mutually surrendered in perfect community. Everything is in common—life, power, truth, happiness—so perfectly indeed that there is no longer simply a possession of the same object, but the existence of identical life, and the community is an identity of the same substance and the same nature.

This divine community is externalized in the Church. For what is it that we then possess in common? What is that All which we receive and give? It is nothing less than the everlasting life of God, in which we are "given a share" through the mystery of regeneration, and which ever and again flows into us in the mystery of the Holy Communion. God is in me, and in you, and in us all. We are all born again from the Father, in Christ, through the Holy Spirit. He is in us, and we in Him. Only read those wonderful chapters of St. John which speak of this mystery, Our Lord's parting discourse to His disciples.

Yet all this is but feeble words. No human utterance can go further. At this point we may quote the final words of St. Bonaventure's treatise on the Ascent of the Spirit in God—*Itinerarium Mentis in Deum*—when he tells his readers: "If you desire further knowledge, question silence, not speech; desire not the understanding; the heartfelt utterance of prayer, not reading and study; the bridegroom, not the teacher; God, not men; darkness, not daylight. Do not question light, but fire, the fire which kindles every heart it touches to a flame that rises up to God in the ecstasy of an overflowing heart and burning Love."

This infinite mystery of truth which has become love, of a possession which belongs to all, this community without limit or end, this giving without reserve— that is the Church, the earthly extension of the divine community, the reflection of God's mutual self-donation. In his last work, which death did not allow him to finish, the *Collationes in Hexameron*, St. Bonaventure has spoken most illuminatingly of this mystery. And you may gather further light from Scheeben's *Mysterien des Christentums* [*Mysteries of the Christian Faith*].

We have followed the mystery of society to its fountainhead—God. There, too, however, we find a counterpart to this society, namely, self-maintenance.

The Father bestows all things upon the Son, and Father and Son all things upon the Holy Spirit. All but one thing—the personal self. That remains immutably contained in itself. Personal unity, the dignity and sublimity of the self, can never be given away. In the process of mutual donation, in the excess of unity, we behold a point of rest, something abiding, surrounded by an impenetrable and sacred circle. It is personality. It can neither be given nor received. It rests in itself. In the very heart of the perfect society it stands alone, fixed in itself. This constitutes its essential inviolability. This inviolability of the person has its counterpart in God's relations with man. To be sure we all possess the same God. To every man He gives Himself and His entire self. But He gives Himself to each in a unique fashion, corresponding to his unique personality. In God we are all one, members of a community indescribably close. But at the same time each may be sure that God belongs to him in different fashion from that in which He belongs to anyone else, and that in this relationship, he is alone with God. The value of friendship is diminished when it is shared with many. But I know that God—and this is the miracle of His infinite life—belongs to all, but to each in a unique fashion. The holy circle of pure isolation surrounds that peace in which a man's inmost self is alone with his God.

And this law is repeated in every community worthy of the name. This is a truth of the first importance. A profound communal solidarity unites all the members of the Church, but in it the individual is never swallowed up in a featureless identity. It is often said that the communal life of the Church is cold. It is we who are cold, because we are still individualists. We all of us continue the frigid isolation of the social contract and the machine. But we desire to become wholly Catholic. Then, indeed, we shall experience the meaning of community. Then we shall become conscious of a living current passing from man to man, of the pulse throbbing from the heart of Christ through all His members. And yet that hallowed circle will always surround the inmost sanctuary and keep it inviolate. No one will be permitted to approach another too closely, to force his way into another man's soul, to lay a hand upon his inner independence, or override it. A profound reverence for human personality will govern everything. For it is the foundation of the Catholic style, whether solemn or joyful, in the Catholic manner of making requests or giving presents, the Catholic way of looking at things, the Catholic attitude: in short, of everything truly Catholic.[2]

Catholic commands are always inspired by reverence for their subject. They are based upon the knowledge that personality is sacred. To command in the

Catholic style demands humility, not only from the man who obeys, but from the man who gives the command. It rejects violence, and the more completely, the more defenseless the subordinate in question. The Catholic superior knows that he is the servant of God's authority, and that it is his duty to increase by degrees the independence of his subordinates, and so make them as free as himself.

Catholic obedience is always dignified. It is not obsequious, or a weak leaning on the support of another, but the free and honorable submission to that reasonable obedience, in which the subject knows its limits, and keeps his own independence.

The Catholic way of sharing with others, of giving and receiving, is chaste. It never surrenders the final independence of the person, never breaks down that holy peace within which the soul enjoys her deepest community life, alone with God.

Catholic charity gives help, without wounding the recipient's dignity.

Catholic friendship recognizes this mystery, and ensures that the parties to it always remain new to each other.

Catholic marriage is the perfect isolation of two human beings, and this is the source of its perennial youth.

All this is a sublime ideal. But it is the very soul of Catholic community life.

At Rothenfels one of those present remarked, "Our fellowship must be such that its members are prepared if necessary to give and sacrifice all for each other. Nevertheless it does not proceed directly from man to man—that is the nature of fellowship in which free individuals bind themselves to their fellows by ties of friendship or love—but from me to God, and from God to you." These words were spoken of a particular association. But they state a law which applies in some degree to every true community—however complete it may be, personality must remain inviolate. All community life presupposes this inner isolation.

And it is also the beginning and the end of form. For form signifies that there is a genuine community, but that it is limited in every direction by a consciousness of inner difference between man and man. Forms are but ways in which this fundamental attitude finds an appropriate expression in the various manifestations of community life, and becomes the law which preserves that life from corruption.

The road towards this goal, however, and not only for the elite alone, but for every man of good will, is the Church. She makes it possible for "all" to "be one," and "have all things common." And she also brings home to us as a living conviction the fact that it does not profit a man "if he gain the whole world and suffer the loss of his own soul."

ROMANO GUARDINI

Notes

1. Translator's Note: The Quickborn Association of Catholic Youth was founded in 1910 with Burg Rothenfels a. Main as its headquarters. Its aim is the permeation of the whole of life, literature, and art, with the Catholic spirit. In 1921 it numbered about 6,000 members.

2. I should like here to sketch another line of thought. Catholicism regards every human being as the child of God. In this respect all are fundamentally equal. It is the human being alone that counts in all the essential religious relationships, such as in the Sacrifice of the Mass and in the Sacraments, in the approach to the various religious activities and responsibilities. I do not know if any other social organization besides the Church exists, in which men meet so naturally as man to man, even if one of the parties is an officer of the society. In Confession, for instance, both priest and penitent are removed from their respective social positions and confront each other in their essential characters. Within the spiritual sphere of the Church "the soul," "the human being," "the priest," "the sinner," "the man," "the woman," are in evidence, in short the entire collection of essential human types and aspects detached from their social environment. And this as a matter of course. Once the threshold of the Church is crossed, the fundamental categories of humanity occupy the scene. A simplification of the personality is effected. It is reduced to its essential human elements, cleared of all the obscurations introduced by human imperfections or the influences of a particular epoch. In this consists that unique sense of equality in the Church, which is the more perfect, because it passes without special notice.

On the other hand, the Church is the uncompromising foe of the "democratic" spirit, which would obliterate all distinctions of rank and natural capacity. In this sense she is whole-heartedly aristocratic. This is indeed involved in the tremendous power of tradition. "Democratism"—not democracy—is a wholly modern conception and a novelty. It makes genuine choice, valuation, and testing impossible. The power of tradition, on the contrary, compels the present to submit to a test and rejects those factors which are not strong enough to endure it. Kierkegaard's *Buch über Adler* has brought out in a very remarkable manner this selective and testing force of tradition. Authority also is aristocratic, if it really possesses the courage and strength to rule, and is not merely disguised weakness. The "democratistic" attitude of mind can neither command, nor obey.

Moreover, the Church, by her teaching and institutional embodiment of the evangelical counsels, has set before each one of us the possibility of an extraordinary vocation. She is charged with having established a double morality, one is more easy-going for the world and the other is more lofty for the cloister. If old historical prejudices and scarcely disguised hatred did not stand in the way, it would soon be recognized that this economy is alone in accordance with man's nature. From every man the Church requires perfection—that is to say, with all his strength he must love God, do His will, and work for His Kingdom in his particular sphere. She exhorts every man to grow more and more deeply into God, and so by degrees to make his entire life the service of God, until he can truly say, "I live, now not I: but Christ lives in me."

This is the Christian attitude to life. It admits, however, an essential difference in the rule of life which gives it practical embodiment. The Christian attitude is the readiness to follow the path to which God is calling. But He does not call all by the same road. The majority He calls to follow the ordinary, a few the extraordinary road. The ordinary rule of life is that in which the natural and supernatural values and demands are brought into a harmonious balance. The extraordinary rule of life is that in which even in the external conduct of life everything is directed immediately to the supernatural. The former commanded; the latter counseled. The former is open to all men, the latter only to those "who can take it." To deny that there is any difference between the two rules of life is to deny the actual conditions of human existence. And it is untrue to say that every man is suited to the extraordinary path. It is untrue even in the natural sphere; how much more therefore in the religious. It is Philistinism and democratism which demand the abolition of the extraordinary rule of life, that the follower of the ordinary path may not suffer from a sense of inferiority. On the other hand it is fantastic—and an extremely foolish and dangerous fantasy, too—to maintain that all are called to follow the extraordinary path. Everyone who has once considered what this implies will agree. The Church distinguishes the two rules. This expresses her aristocratic attitude, which refuses to surrender to any cravings for equality.

Yet we can show that it is precisely by this distinction that each rule of life makes the full development of the other possible, so that the complete structure of human life can be built up. The rule of life in which the extraordinary principle finds objective expression is that of the evangelical counsels—poverty, chastity, and obedience. These are means by which man in the concrete wholly transfers the momentum of his life to God, places surrender at every point above self-preservation, the supernatural above the natural. Actually the way of life resulting from these counsels can either be followed freely "in the world," or else in the regulated forms represented by religious orders. What, then, is the significance of the latter for the community?

I am leaving out of account here the actual services they perform, for example their care of the poor and the sick, the intercession for the community made by the religious rule, who in their contemplation present the entire human race to God. I am concerned solely with the consideration of their sociological effect. The extraordinary fact of a perfect voluntary renunciation—and not as an ephemeral exception, but as a perpetual phenomenon—gives that great majority who follow the ordinary path, that independence of the possessions concerned, which is the more indispensable perquisite of their right use.

To take one instance: marriage is the isolation of two persons in God, and as a form of community, which is more than the mere sum of two partners and something higher, the image of God's Kingdom, the Church, and in every aspect as a fertility duly ordered. As such it cannot be established merely upon the basis on those natural forces which tend towards marriage (To many this

THE MEANING OF THE CHURCH

may seem a paradox—and it is. But when we have long pondered the forms of human life; the relation between their aims arising from their very nature and the forces actually at their disposal, the relation between one form and another; and the intrinsic economy of life, we come to understand that what superficially seems a paradox is often the only truly natural thing. Paradox is embedded in the very heart of normality. It is so here.) The forces which normally produce marriage are insufficient to make a marriage which fulfills its own inner nature. Such a marriage requires a perfect capacity of assent and surrender, but also an equally great independence of the sexual factor. Without the former the union is too superficial; without the latter it lacks inner dignity and the capacity for fidelity. Nature, however cannot by itself produce this. It is only that perfect surrender in the conduct of life, which "thinks only of the things that are God's," which, by the constant influence it has exerted upon others through the centuries, awakens in the married also the strength requisite for complete surrender, with all the sacrifices that this entails. And their total renunciation of sex creates that freedom from the excessive power of sex, which in its turn reacts upon the mass of men and women and alone can make marriage faithful and chaste. To deny the possibility of this renunciation and surrender to God is also to deny man's noblest capacities and shake the foundation of true marriage. On the other hand, if a renunciation is to be truly heroic, the thing renounced must admittedly be valuable. An epoch must be fully aware of the value of marriage, of the treasures it comprises, if the sacrifice of the celibate is to be seen as something truly extraordinary. Marriage must display that profound inner wealth, must possess that nobility, must be that miraculous product fashioned by the cooperation of natural and supernatural forces, which Christ willed, Paul suggested, and the Church has always cherished. For the distinctive sacrifice in virginity is its renunciation of the perfect community and creative powers which only marriage can produce. Thus the loneliness of the extraordinary path can alone ensure that the rule, namely, marriage, shall become noble and profound. But conversely only marriage makes that sacrifice what it must be, if it is to realize the values inherent in its nature. Marriage, too need be heroic, if the life of virginity is to escape the danger of becoming commonplace. The extraordinary is not heroic simply as such. On the contrary, it consists in the perfect purity, generosity, and fidelity with which the extraordinary vocation is fulfilled. Similarly, the ordinary is not of its nature commonplace. It also becomes heroic when it is realized with perfect purity, courage and fidelity.

We must not confuse the characteristic distinctions between the two ways with distinctions of moral dispositions. There "extraordinary" may also be very "commonplace," the ordinary very heroic. Marriage and virginity or more generally—the rule and the exception—duty and counsel—are forms of Christian life. "Mediocre" and "heroic," on the contrary, are attitudes towards life. Every form of life can be lived in n heroic or in a mediocre spirit. And the resolve to live a life of heroic and unreserved self-devotion does not of itself determine the form of life in which it shall be accomplished. The "good will" decides the former choice, "vocation" the latter. We need men and women to live the extraordinary form of life heroically. But we have just as great need of others to live the ordinary form of life heroically. Heroism in marriage is just as indispensable as heroism in virginity. And it is certain that both types of heroism, viewed from the sociological standpoint, mutually support each other. So deeply are aristocracy and—the right term does not exist—democracy interwoven in the Catholic spiritual order. Those who take the right point of view will observe at every turn, with a delight mingled with a certain awe, how marvelously, how even uncannily right the Church is in all her values and arrangements; and how her attitude so commonly charged with hostility to life is in complete accord with life's most profound demands. We have, indeed, good cause to trust the Church! We have but to encounter such a masterpiece of the divine penetration and fashioning of human life, and all objections vanish into thin air.

Epilogue

These lectures have not attempted to establish by scientific reasoning, but to state as my firm conviction, that the sphere of Catholic faith—the Church—is not merely one alternative among many, but religious truth, pure and simple, the Kingdom of God. The Church is not something belonging to the past, but absolute reality, and therefore the answer to every age, including our own, and its fulfillment. And this fulfillment will be the more perfect, the more substantial, and the more complete our acceptance of the reality displayed by the Catholic faith and the more serious our endeavor to make our own the spiritual disposition it involves. This genuine Catholicity, which is seriously convinced of the supernatural and dogmatic character of Catholicism, is the most open-minded and the most comprehensive attitude, or rather the only open-minded comprehensive attitude, in existence. If by open-mindedness we mean the intellectual outlook which sees and values all objects as they really are, the Church can claim this description, because in face of the superabundant wealth of human experience she occupies the sole perfectly stable, clear and determined position. Both the wealth and the fixity enter into the Catholic mind. For the man whose outlook is narrow and timid and whose experience of reality is impoverished, falls as far short of the Catholic outlook as the man who is incapable of an unconditional affirmative or negative, or who waters down her definitely supernatural teaching, or explains away the clear historical facts upon which it is based.

But more remains to be said. Already in my second lecture I pointed out that we are concerned with the actual, not the ideal Church, not with a spiritual one, but the historical Church as she exists today. The Church is not an ideal, which can be constructed a priori, and upon which we may fall back when reality fails us, as, for instance, we may elaborate an ideal state. Fundamentally there is no such thing as a philosophy of the Church. She is, on the contrary, a unique fact. Her position in this respect resembles that of a man. If anyone were to say that a particular judgment was applicable not to his friend in the concrete, but only to his ideal, and in consequence were to divert his approval from the man to the ideal, he would be guilty of an injustice to his friend's personality. It would indeed be worse than an injustice; it would be disloyalty. For it would be a complete blindness to the essential decision with which human personality confronts us to accept or refuse it as it actually is. It demands yes or no, hostility or loyalty, but cannot admit a retreat into the abstract and a denial of reality in the name of the ideal. Such an attribute would be metaphysically false, because it would ignore the essential nature of individual personality by treating it as nothing more than a particular instance of a universal, and it would be morally unacceptable, because it would substitute for the attitude which must be adopted towards a person the attitude proper in the case of a mere thing. It is equally irrational to distinguish between the reality and the ideal of the Church. This, however, makes a further distinction the more indispensable. We must inquire whether the real inner form of the Church, her inner perfection ordained by God, is revealed by any given external of manifestation. Are forces which spring from her very essence fully operative in the visible expressions of her life? Is her inner nature visible in her members? No one can evade this question, for it concerns each one of us personally. When a man reaches the conviction that the Church is absolute in her actual nature and in every age teaches the way to perfection and the strength by which it may be achieved, his immediate reaction will be an intense gratitude. But this gratitude must not induce him to settle down in spiritual comfort, but must be felt as a demand. The parable of the talents is applicable also to our relation to the Church. We are all responsible for her, each in his own way, the priest in virtue of his ordination, the layman in virtue of his Confirmation. Upon each one of us depends the degree of harmony achieved between the nature of the Church and her outward semblance, between her inner and outer aspects. Here, too, we bear a heavy responsibility towards those outside the Church. It requires the vision of love and of faith to see the inner nature of the Church beneath expressions often so defective. Even her own members sometimes lack this vision. How much less then is it to be expected from those who regard the Church with distrust as strangers, blinded by the prejudices and false values of their education! We cannot blame them if they regard the assertions made in these lectures as theorizing. For it is indeed true that a valid argument in this sphere should be conducted by Catholics, whose lives inspire confidence. Their proofs, it is true, are not without their intrinsic value. But their power to bring conviction is strongest when they are supported by a living "proof of power."

PANGUR BÁN

Designed by Fiona Cecile Clarke, the CLUNY MEDIA *logo*
depicts a monk at work in the scriptorium,
with a cat sitting at his feet.

The monk represents our mission to emulate
the invaluable contributions of the monks
of Cluny in preserving the libraries of the West,
our strivings to know and love the truth.

The cat at the monk's feet is Pangur Bán, from the
eponymous Irish poem of the 9th century.
The anonymous poet compares his scholarly
pursuit of truth with the cat's happy hunting of mice.
The depiction of Pangur Bán is an homage to the work
of the monks of Irish monasteries and a sign
of the joy we at Cluny take in our trade.

"Messe ocus Pangur Bán,
cechtar nathar fria saindan:
bíth a menmasam fri seilgg,
mu memna céin im saincheirdd."

CPSIA information can be obtained
at www.ICGtesting.com
Printed in the USA
FSHW021824150220
67053FS